Title: You're Never Too Old To Quilt
Copyright: Christine Sutton 2022
ISBN 978-0-64518-79-9-9
Published by M.C. Sutton Publishing,
139/218 Bishop Rd, Beachmere, 4510

The author asserts her right to be identified as such in accordance with the Copyright Amendment (Disability Access and Other Measures) Act 2017.

Except as otherwise permitted under Copyright Amendment (Disability Access and Other Measures) Act 2017, this publication and/or its contents may only be reproduced, stored or transmitted with the prior permission of the publisher.

Printed in Melbourne Australia by Lightning Source

First Published 2023

Hello from Beachmere!!

I'm Chris Sutton. I'm a Home Based Quilter (HBQ) With my partner, Paul, and our crazy Labradoodle Nicnak Tiger Woods, I live in a Retirement Village in a small coastal town, just north of Brisbane, Queensland.

At 77 years of age, I'm an "Old Chook" (Australian for "old lady"), not that I feel like one! I love retirement. It gives me the freedom to do what, when and where I like - to follow my passions. So, I learn, I teach, I quilt and I write.

Now I don't claim to be an expert quilter, far from it. For me, every day is a learning day. A previous generation of quilters taught and mentored me, and I continue to learn from our global quilting community. Teaching beginners, older "newbies", is the best way of giving back, so I teach Beginners Quilting classes for older learners.

The more I teach, the more concerned I become that we are losing our older quilters. We need them to teach their children, grandchildren and great grandchildren, to sustain a valuable tradition. And we are losing them for all the wrong reasons.

Age can slowly rob us of the pleasure of quilting. My body is experiencing the wear and tear of a busy and full life - and it hurts. If I have physical challenges so do lots of others, and not all are seniors.

There are many, many quilters out there with arthritis, back injuries, carpal tunnel syndrome, Parkinson's Disease and other challenges. It's hard to cut a straight line, stand for long periods cutting fabric or manipulate heavy quilts through a sewing machine.

Quilting is good for us! Quilting has tremendous benefits. Our age related physical challenges shouldn't stop us. When I started on my quilting journey, I was in my 30s. Now I'm on the 80 side of my 70s, with a dicky back, stiff hands and shoulders and a painful hip. Can I still quilt? Will I keep on quilting? Of course! You bet I can! And so can you!

The older I get, the more I value what I can still do despite my ageing body, especially my quilting. I'm still designing and creating as well as, if not better than, I did when I started forty years ago. My secret? It's not rocket science. It's about being adaptable, finding new tools to compensate, and learning new ways of working. In the 2020s, there are tools, techniques and technologies to help us all quilt for so much longer.

I hope you find this book helpful, and discover, as I have, new ways to keep on quilting for as long as you enjoy it.

Happy Quilting

Chris Sutton

P.S. Watch out for the Old Chook Quilter. She's left some great tips & tricks for you.

DEDICATION

This book pays respect to the spirit of quilters who passed down their wisdom and creativity through the generations. We have them to thank for the joys and benefits of quilting.

It recognises the present global community of quilters who follow in the traditions of the past, break new ground, and guide and teach their children, grandchildren and great grandchildren, their friends and communities the skills and joys of quilting.

It thanks, encourages, and urges manufacturers to continue to research and develop tools and technology to allow Old Chooks and Roosters, and Challenged Spring Chickens to quilt and sew with less pain and frustration.

Thank You

Acknowledgements

My heartfelt thanks to ;

Paul Lupi, for your support and care, for putting up with my obsession and keeping me watered and fed while I had my head down and my bottom up working on this book.

Grace Co for creating tools for folks like us. For your support and assistance in supplying information and the Grace and True Cut images with copyright permission to use them. My personal thanks to Justice Daniels, Delaney Nye, and Allegra Erznoznik for their support and assistance.

The members of the QAYG Class at Beachmere Sands Retirement Village, who provide the inspiration for this book and acted as Crash Test Dummies for the block patterns and cutting techniques.

Nanny Leah, who taught me to sew and embroider and passed on her love of fabric arts. She sits on my shoulder and guides me as I stitch. Miss you Nanny! Every day,

All the wise women quilters who over the years have shared their knowledge and skills with me and made me a better quilter than I could have been alone.

Attributions and references

1. **Grace product images** - Grace Co 2225 South 3200 West Salt Lake City, UT 84119 United States

2. **Pixabay** Copyright free images courtesy of Pixabay http://www.pixabay.com

3. "The Synapse Project: Engagement in Mentally Challenging Activities Enhances Neural Efficiency," by Ian M. McDonough, Sara Haber, Gérard N. Bischof, and Denise C. Park. *Restorative Neurology and Neuroscience,* Volume 33, Issue 6 (2015), DOI: 10.3233/RNN-150533, published by IOS Press. Texas

4. Emily L. Burt, Jacqueline Atkinson, **The relationship between quilting and wellbeing,** *Journal of Public Health*, Volume 34, Issue 1, March 2012, Pages 54–59, https://doi.org/10.1093/pubmed/fdr041 Glasgow

5. Dana Howell & Doris Pierce (2000) **Exploring the forgotten restorative dimension of occupation: Quilting and quilt use,** Journal of Occupational Science, 7:2, 68-72, DOI: 10.1080/14427591.2000.9686467

Introduction
The benefits of quilting to over 65s

There is strong evidence, too strong to ignore, that quilting is a desirable and valuable activity to health, well being and maintenance of our social ties and independence as we age.

In 2014 researchers at the University of Texas provided *"...the first experimental evidence that mentally-challenging leisure activities can actually change brain function and that it is possible that such interventions can restore levels of brain activity to a more youth-like state."*

The study involved randomly assigned participants, all of whom were seniors, to three groups; a. high challenge, b. low-challenge and c. no-challenge. The three groups spent at least 15 hours per week for 14 weeks in leisure activities.

- The high-challenge group learning progressively more difficult skills in quilting and/or digital photography.
- The low-challenge group meeting to socialise and engage in activities related to subjects such as travel and cooking (no active learning component).
- The no-challenge group engaging in low-cognitive demand tasks such as listening to music, playing simple games, or watching classic movies.

During the study, all participants had a range of cognitive tests and brain scans using an MRI technology that measures brain activity. These occurred before and after the 14-week period and a subset was retested a year later.

"The high-challenge group showed better memory performance after the intervention, and an increased ability to modulate brain activity more efficiently to challenging judgments of word meaning in the brain areas associated with attention and language processing. Some of this enhanced brain activity was still clear a year later. Participants showed a pattern of response typical of younger adults."
(McDonough, Haber, Bischof, and Park 2015).

Since then, other investigations by British and US neuroscientists, psychologists and Public Health authorities have identified quilting as a highly beneficial activity for older adults.

Neurologists believe quilting involves both logic and creativity - activities that exercise the brain in a unique way, by activating areas of the cerebral cortex that control vision and guide fine motor skills. This "brain exercise" continues throughout the process of making a quilt.

Specialists in ageing and well being not only attribute quilting's benefits for brain health to its relationship with selecting and combining colours and shapes, but also for its restorative benefits for social and emotional health and wellbeing. They well know the physical benefits of quilting to the Over 65s:

- *Quilting lowers heart rate and blood pressure.* Studies have shown that because of the calming effect that these hobbies have on the body and how they can counteract the stress response, quilting can lower heart rate and blood pressure. Good news those who suffer from these common conditions. It also means that quilting might be an effective form of therapy.

- It reduces risk of dementia and loss of brain function. Recent studies looked at various hobbies and whether they helped reduce the risk of dementia and preserve brain function. It found people who learnt quilting, were 45% less likely to suffer from mild cognitive impairment. It's thought that the physical and mental stimulation of the brain may increase growth factors that help brain cells function better and prevent them from dying.

- Quilting improves hand eye coordination This is important for a variety of reasons, including preventing falls. Research has shown that as we age, our ability to perform ordinary manual tasks declines. The decline in hand-eye coordination can cause an annoying increase in 'clumsiness', something we don't think about, until we have a problem. Taking steps that can help prevent health problems like this is always preferable to treatment, especially if the activity is enjoyable, like quilting.

- It increases activity and flexibility. providing movement your body needs to stay healthy. It involves a surprising amount of movement, especially when compared to sitting and watching the television or playing board games. Laying out fabric, cutting and working your sewing machine are all beneficial. The skills needed for quilting all help to stretch the muscles of the hands, arms and shoulders naturally, helping us retain flexibility and suppleness.

Quilting also has mental health benefits.

- There is a feeling of accomplishment that comes with completing something that helps alleviate depression. IT comes when you show your finished quilt to others. Whether you share it with a quilting group or online - it feels great!

- Social benefits come with quilting. One of the best things about quilting is the people we meet. Quilters interact with people from all walks of life and backgrounds who become new friends. Joining a quilting group is a great way to meet like-minded people and learn heaps, especially if you are a newbie.

- It can deliver or rekindle a sense of purpose. Quilting for charity is a wonderful way to use your creative skills and gives you a sense of purpose.

- Quilting can be a huge stress relief. Whether or not we realise it, sometimes we are under excessive stress. Having a pastime like quilting can help reduce the feeling of being overwhelmed. Quilting forces you to focus on one thing, disengaging the brain from stressful thoughts and feelings.

- It fosters mindfulness. We learn more every day about 'mindfulness', living in the present moment, without judgement. It has amazing benefits. Although many people use meditation, you can still experience many of the benefits of mindfulness by focussing on an absorbing pastime like quilting.

Research is all fine, and it's good to have proof of what quilters have known for many years. Those of us who are old quilting chooks and roosters already recognise the benefits and know quilting helps us to live well, mentally, physically and emotionally.

However, try as we might we can't control the effects age has on our body as the years go by.

For some of us, physical ageing can be a challenge, if not a barrier, to continuing to quilt. As we grow older, hand quilting and machine quilting become difficult as our fingers, hands, shoulders and backs begin to stiffen or become painful through arthritis.

Age affects our physical ability to hold and use quilting tools and manipulate the weight of large quilts.

We dread the time when we can no longer enjoy our well loved pastime.

There's good news!
There are now tools and techniques to keep us quilting despite our aches and pains and challenges.

This book is for you who love quilting and want to keep on quilting forever, and for you who have never quilted but would like to take it up and reap its rewards.

Based on "QuiltAs-You-Go" methods, it identifies tools and techniques the design of which make cutting, sewing and manipulating the fabric easier for older hands and backs.

No matter whether the challenges of ageing are restricting your enjoyment of quilting, or you are coming to quilting for the first time in your senior years, there are ideas in this book to foster the love and joy of patchwork and quilting and encourage quilters to keep on doing what they love.

Whether alone in your happy place at home, or with a group of like-minded friends, you are never too old to quilt!

Contents

Start here!	14
What is Quilting?	15
The Language of Quilting	19
The best tools for a painless project	27
For Beginners- start with basic tools	28
Rotary Cutters for problem hands and wrists	29
Cutting mats	31
Rotating cutting mat	32
Rulers	33
Rulers for senior hands	34
Scissors and other essential cutters	35
Fabric cutting machines	38
Sewing machines	42
Irons and ironing boards	47
Be it ever so humble... Your Happy Place	51
Room to quilt and sew	52
Understanding Colour	59
Hues, tints, shades and tones.	61
Using the Colour Wheel	62
Applying the color wheel to fabric choice	64
Colour Tools	66

Fabric — 69
Batting — 73
Haberdashery — 77

Creating a Quilt — 81
The Golden Rules of Cutting — 86
Cutting — 86
Putting the rules to work. — 91
Piecing the quilt — 93

Let's make a small quilt — 95
The quilting skills you have mastered. — 104

Clever cuts and Beaut Blocks — 105
Short cuts to pieced patches — 106
Half Square Triangle Short Method — 106
A Modern Star — 108
Quarter Square Triangles — 109
3-Patch Quarter Square Triangle — 110
3-Patch Quarter Square Triangle — 112
Flying Geese — 114
Martha Washington's Star — 118
How put a triangle onto a rectangle. — 120
Sawtooth Block — 121
Cutting "One Way" Trapezoids — 122

Double Pinwheel Block	124
A word about squaring up blocks	126
Block 1 - Simple Four Patch	128
Block 2 - Disappearing 4 Patch	129
Block 3 - Disappearing 9 Patch	130
Double Disappearing 9 Patch.	131
Block 4 - Log Cabin	134
Block 5 - The Manx Quilt	138
Block 6 - Martha Washington's Star	142
Traditional Sawtooth Block	145

Quilt As You Go — 147

What is QAYG?	148
QAYG, step by step.	148
QAYG Variations	158
Different kinds of sashing	159

Quilting — 163

Why quilt?	164
Preparation	164
Basting	165
Quilting	165
Straight line quilting	165
Controlled quilting	166

	Free motion quilting	169
	Quilting frames	173
Useful Stuff		177
Glossary of Terms		180

Start here!

If you are over 50 years old, can you still learn to quilt? Of course you can. The right tools and techniques will have you proudly gifting beautiful quilts to friends and family, made with love.

Whatever your age, if there are physical impairments limiting your ability to stitch and manipulate large sewing projects, with the right tools and know-how, you can learn to quilt and keep on quilting, even when the strength and mobility of your body presents challenges.

As you work your way through this book, you will find the knowledge and skills, tricks and tips to make your quilting life easier, together with some basic projects to start you off. With *"You're Never Too Old To Quilt"* you will be able to;

- Understand what quilting is and where it came from, how patchwork and quilting work together and what the Quilt-As-You-Go method does for seniors and physically challenged quilters.

- Understand the language and acronyms of quilting,

- Identify the tools and equipment you need to get started in quilting, particularly those that make measuring and cutting easier if you have back or mobility problems or arthritic hands.

Find answers to questions like "What kind of fabric should I use? What are pre-cuts? How do I work out how much fabric I need? Where can I buy fabric?

- Make your first quilted project, using step by step instructions, and clear diagrams and photos.

- Make quilt blocks using Quilt-As-You-Go methods and join the blocks and rows to complete your quilt.

- Make traditional blocks for quilts, together with nifty tricks to make them easier.

- Follow a quilt pattern to construct a quilt using QAYG and traditional quilt blocks.

- Identify quilting accessories to take your machine quilting to the next level should you wish to do so.

What is Quilting?

If you were to ask my partner that question he would probably answer, *"It's cutting stuff into little pieces and sewing them back together again."* Which is the kind of reply I give when asked "What is golf? " - *"A long walk chasing a little white ball around a winding garden with holes in it."* True, but there's a lot more to it.

Quilting is a method of stitching layers of fabric together in layers. We call this a "sandwich", for obvious reasons.

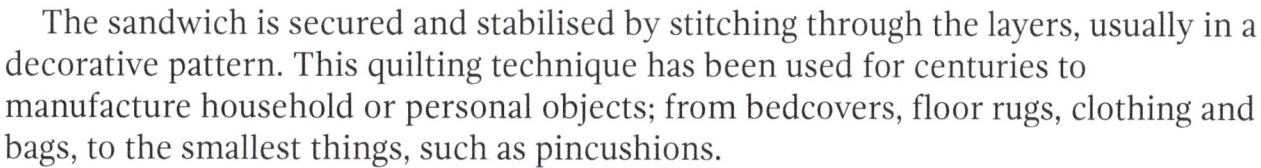

There are usually three layers;

- A top layer of patchworked fabrics, the part that will be seen if it is a bed quilt, a table topper or a place mat,
- A middle layer of batting or insulating material
- A bottom layer of fabric.

The sandwich is secured and stabilised by stitching through the layers, usually in a decorative pattern. This quilting technique has been used for centuries to manufacture household or personal objects; from bedcovers, floor rugs, clothing and bags, to the smallest things, such as pincushions.

Are quilting and patchwork the same?

No. Patchwork is the art of sewing pieces of fabric together to form a pattern . Originally it was a way of using up scraps of fabrics or of extending the working life of clothing, now we use it most often as the top layer of a quilted item.

However, most quilters combine the two techniques, using various tools to measure and cut the fabrics and stitch the assembled quilt using the patchwork as the top layer.

So what is the difference? A quilter may work with a single piece of fabric on the top layer and another on the bottom, or the same fabric top and bottom. Quilting is the technique used to stitch the three layers together.

A brief history of quilting

The history of quilting may date back as far as 3400 BCE, (Solis-Cohen, 1993). We know quilting existed in Europe around the beginning of the 13th century AD, during the Crusades. The Turkish army wore several thicknesses of fabric quilted together under their armour. In northern Europe's harsh climate, quilting offered warmth and protection not only beneath metal armour, but also in bedcovers and various forms of clothing. Archaeologists found small fragments of patchwork in tomb excavations in Asia and the Middle East. The oldest surviving example of a quilted piece is a linen carpet found in a Mongolian cave, dated to between 100 BC and 200AD.

The earliest existing European quilts may be two large 13th-century Sicilian pieces whose surfaces are heavily embellished with trapunto, (stuffed) quilting. One quilt is in the collection of the Victoria and Albert Museum in London, the other in the Bargello Museum in Florence. Both depict scenes from the legend of Tristan and Isolde. The expertise displayed in these demonstrates they were part of an accomplished and highly evolved craft. Originally, quilters worked by hand. Today the art is practiced by both hand and machine quilters and is recognised as a pastime that has great benefit to cognitive developed and healthy ageing.

Manx Quilting

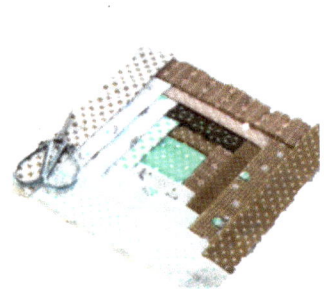

The quilters of the Isle of Man, a small island situated in the Irish Sea, half way between England and Ireland, still practice an ancient form of quilting. The island is so tiny and so isolated that almost everything needed to make clothing, houses and furniture must be brought in by ship. Manx quilting came from the need to reuse and repurpose fabrics from worn clothing, bedclothes and packaging materials such as hessian. Similar to a log cabin block, the pieces are torn from scraps of material and hand sewn with needle and thread. Rulers, cutting tools and machines are not needed,

Later in this book you will find instructions on how to make a Manx block.

Why quilt?

There are lots of reasons why we quilt. Most are very personal . You'll often hear quilters say that their pastime takes them to their "happy place". It's relaxing, they become lost in the processes. Quilting requires concentration and creativity. I started quilting for many of the same reasons I hear from my quilting friends around the world, but there is another reason why I quilt. I believe that quilting is one of the most valuable pastimes for our ageing population, one that will help us age well? Easy! The research tells us so.

Quilting exercises the brain uniquely, by activating areas of the brain that control vision, guide fine motor skills and understand words and how to use them. When you are in the middle of a quilt, you must concentrate and focus.

Why quilt-as-you-go?

There are three groups of quilters, hand quilters, machine quilters and those who use one or both styles together with the quilt-as-you-go methods.

- Hand quilters sew everything by hand, including all over quilting bed quilts, baby blankets and large quilted pieces. This involves lifting and holding heavy pieces as they sew.

- Machine quilters sew their quilts on an ordinary domestic sewing machine. Once the top is made, they have to manipulate the batting and backing, lay it out on a table, or if it's a bed quilt, the floor, pin the layers in place and then manhandle the huge sandwich through the sewing machine to quilt and bind it.

- Quilt-as-you-go involves making and quilting a project block by block and then joining the blocks together, first in strips, and then joining the strips together to form the completed quilt. The quilting is already completed, block by block so there is no need to manhandle large quilts through the sewing machine until the very end, when you join two halves together with a sashing strip.

As we grow older, quilting by traditional methods may become difficult as our fingers, hands, shoulders and backs stiffen or become painful through arthritis, and other ageing issues affect our ability to hold and use fine sewing implements and manipulate the weight of a large quilt. This is when Quilt-as -you-go allows us to continue to create our quilts with love but without pain for as long as possible.

Measurements

While our measuring systems are decimal, quilting measurements are imperial, that is, inches, feet and yards. Why? The USA is the traditional "home" of modern quilting. Most of our traditional blocks and quilt patterns come from there. The USA still uses the imperial system, therefore so do quilters.

Most Australian and British senior quilters have no problems with the Imperial system. We grew up with it, so measurements in quilting are a doddle.

I can still recite the table;

12 inches (12") = 1 foot   3 feet (ft) = 1 yd

I have old tape measures and school rulers in inches, and some in both inches and centimetres. Anyone too young to remember the old measurements has the problem of translating patterns containing imperial cutting guides and fabric needs into decimals .

Our problem is translating decimals into inches and yards, because where we live governs how fabric, bed sizes and block sizes are sold and measured. In Australia we use decimal measurements, meaning fabric is sold in cm and metres.

No matter whether you are most comfortable with decimals or imperial measures, every quilter needs to be able convert backwards and forwards, either to follow a pattern, to create the right size quilt or purchase fabric.

The solution is to keep a calculator handy when you are working out how much fabric you will need, or make friends with your local quilting and fabric shop. They will be only too pleased to help you.

Some useful facts;

- To convert centimetres to inches, divide by 2.54
- A quick estimate - 12" is roughly 31cm. Therefore your 30cm ruler is a little longer than the old 12 inch ruler.
- A yard is approximately 95cm. When the pattern calls for a yard of fabric and you buy a metre, you'll have a little more than you need. If it says 5 yards of fabric and you buy 5 metres, you'll have a quarter of a metre (25 cm) too much.

Here are some useful free mobile apps and websites that will help you;

- Robert Kaufman QuiltingCalc - Google Play or Apple Store
- Quilters Paradise website - https://www.quiltersparadiseesc.com/Calculators.php
- The Strawberry Thief website = https://thestrawberrythief.com.au/fabric-calculators/

The Language of Quilting

Understanding the language of quilting is a big help when you go shopping for fabric or tools, and especially when you are following a pattern for a block or quilt. Here's a basic list of terms you need to know now. At the back of the book you will find a more extensive glossary.

APPLIQUÉ

A technique where fabric shapes are sewn onto a fabric block or quilt top. A fusible material is ironed to the wrong side of a shape, and ironed to the background fabric. Needle turned: this involves hand work where you use a needle to turn edge under and then hand stitch in place. Raw edge appliqué: technique used to fuse your shape to fabric, then use a decorative stitch to adhere to quilt block.

BASTING

Joining layers of fabric or the layers of a quilt with safety pins or large stitches. The stitching is temporary and is removed after permanent stitching. Pin-basting is accomplished using quilting safety pins to hold layers together.

BATTING

A non-woven textile used between two pieces of fabric to form a quilt. The thickness and fibre vary and include cotton, wool and polyester blends.

BIAS

The grain of woven fabric that is at a 45° angle to the selvages.

BINDING

Finishing of the quilt. Long, thin fabric strips that are attached to the raw edges of a quilt.

BLOCKS

The unit that is designed for a quilt. Generally, there will be many blocks in a quilt. A quilt block can be a single piece of fabric cut with a rotary cutter into a square or a block that has been pieced using many pieces of fabric and sewn together using ¼ inch seam allowance.

BORDER

Strips of fabric that frame the edges of the quilt. You may also have borders surrounding your quilt blocks, also known as sashing.

CHAIN-PIECING OR CHAINING

Sewing a pair of fabric pieces together and continuously pushing pairs under the presser foot without cutting the thread between them.

CHARM PACK

A variety of a fabric line cut into 5″ squares. Number in bundles can vary among manufacturers.

CORNERSTONE

A fabric square positioned at the corner of sashing strips, or a plain square or pieced block used in the four corners of a quilt border.

CORNER TRIANGLE

The triangles set in the corners of a quilt that is set on "Point." These are half square triangles, meaning the straight of grain is on the outer edges of the triangle.

ECHO QUILTING

Outline quilting around an appliqué. The first line of quilting is quilted in-the-ditch of the appliqué. The next line is quilted a set gap away e.g. 1" from the first, and from then the gap is ½"

FAT QUARTER or FAT FLAT

A rectangle of fabric measuring approximately 45cm x 52 cm . It is one of four equal rectangles cut from a metre length of fabric. In countries using the Imperial measurement system, a Fat Quarter/Flat is usually a yard cut into four rectangles, each of which is approximately 18" x 20".

FEED DOGS

Teeth like mechanisms that sits below the presser foot of a sewing machine and move fabric through the machine as you stitch. Feed dogs also help control stitch length. If you drop your feed dogs, you can achieve free motion quilting.

FINGER-PRESSING

Pressing fabric between your fingers to make a temporary crease.

FINISHED SIZE

The measurement of a completed block that has been sewn into a quilt.

FREE MOTION QUILTING

A process requiring a free motion quilting, darning or hopping foot. Requires you to drop your feed dogs so you can move fabric freely in all directions. Special gloves marketed for free motion quilting can help in controlling the fabric by providing extra grip.

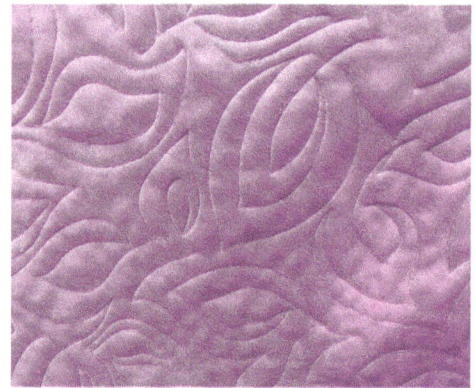

GRAIN

The direction of woven fabric. The cross grain is from selvedge to selvedge. The lengthwise grain runs parallel to the selvedge and is stronger. The bias grain runs at 45° and has the greatest stretch.

HALF SQUARE TRIANGLE

Acronym - HST

A triangle that is created when you cut a square from one corner to opposite corner (45-degree angle). Straight of grain is on the short, outer sides of the triangle.

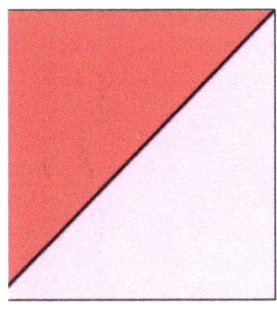 

IN-THE-DITCH QUILTING

The top stitching that is made alongside a seam, usually on the side without the seam allowance.

JELLY ROLL

Fabric cut into 2 ½ inch strips and wound into a roll. Used for strip piecing and other various patterns, and also binding.

LAYER CAKE

Fabric that is cut into 10" squares.

LOFT

Loft means thickness. The higher the batting loft , the thicker the quilt. Thicker batting is more difficult to baste. There are battings that are very thin and super warm.

MITRED SEAM

A 45° angle seam.

OUTLINE QUILTING

Stitching that is made outside or inside the pieced seam lines of patchwork.

PATCHWORK

A composite of pieces sewn together to form a larger piece, such as a block or quilt.

PIECING

Process where fabric pieces are sewn together to form a block, garment or quilt.

PRESSING

Using an iron with an up and down motion to set stitches and flatten seam allowances.

QST - quarter square triangle

QUARTER INCH FOOT

Presser foot that has a guide to achieve a ¼ inch seam.

QAYG

Quilt As You Go

QUARTER SQUARE TRIANGLE

Acronym - QST

Triangle made when you cut a square diagonally twice from corner to opposite corner at 45 degree angles, making an X in centre of block. Straight grain will be on long edge of triangle. You will obtain 4 triangles from one square.

QUILT AS YOU GO

Process where each block or section is layered and quilted separately. Each separately quilted block or section is then be assembled into a larger quilt.

QUILTING

The small running stitches made through the layers of a quilt (quilt top, batting and backing) to form decorative patterns on the surface of the quilt and hold the layers together.

QUILT SANDWICH

The three layers of a quilt: the quilt top, the quilt batting, the quilt backing.

RAW EDGE

The cut end of fabric.

ROTARY CUTTER

It is a sharp blade wheel, in a handle, used to slice through multiple layers of fabric.

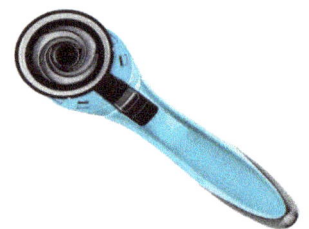

ROTARY-CUTTING

The process of cutting fabric into strips and pieces using a revolving blade rotary cutter, a thick, clear plastic ruler, and a special cutting mat.

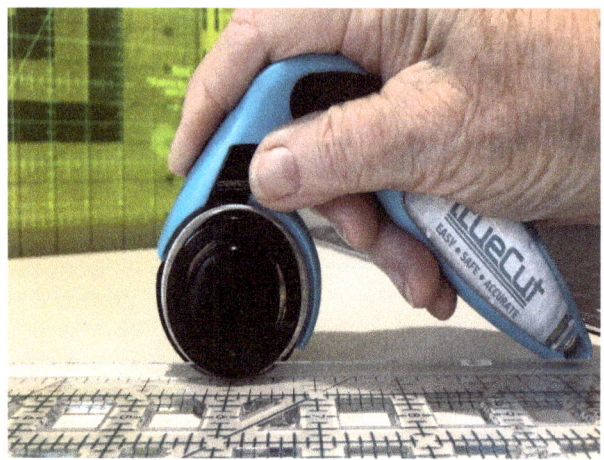

ROTARY MAT

A rotating cutting mat with a surface that is self-healing. Used to cut fabric with rotary cutters. You can turn the fabric without moving it.

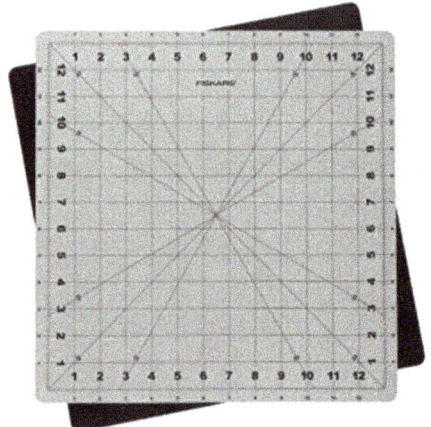

SEAM ALLOWANCE

The margin of fabric between the stitched seam and the raw edge.

SEAM LINE

The guideline that the quilter follows while stitching.

QUARTER INCH SEAM

Sewing instructions often say "sew with a ¼ seam". You can draw a line ¼" from the edge of the piece you are going to join, or use a ¼" foot on your sewing machine. Most brands of sewing machine have a ¼ inch foot as an accessory. Check with your sewing machine supplier or try the Universal ¼" foot available from large sewing supplies retailers.

SELVEDGE / SELVAGE

The tightly woven lengthwise finished edge on each side of the fabric. It prevents the

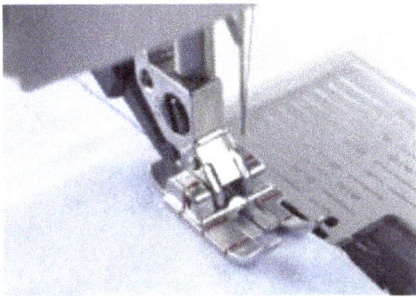

edges from fraying or unravelling.

Some selvedge has information regarding the manufacturer, artist or designer, colour-way and arrows indicating the straight grain of the fabric.

SET OR SETTING

The arrangement of blocks in a quilt top.

SETTING SQUARE

A plain block that's sewn next to 8 pieced block.

SETTING THE SEAM

A seam is pressed on the right side before pressing it to the side/open. Allows the thread to relax into your fabric.

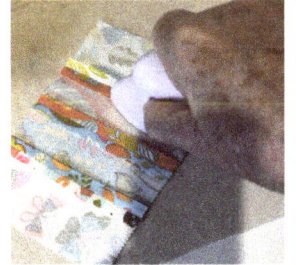

SLIPSTITCH

A hand-stitch used for finishing such as sewing binding to a quilt, or a sleeve to a quilt back.

STASH

Fabrics in your cupboards, under your bed and in plastic storage boxes. They are fabrics collected for quilting projects, left over from a project, patterns you really liked, or because you have a fabric addiction.

STRIP PIECING

A technique where strips are cut and pieced together and then pieced strips are cut to design a block.

STRIP-SETS

Two or more strips of fabric, cut and sewn together along the length of the strips.

SUB-CUT

Cutting fabric strip sets into smaller units.

TIED QUILT

Technique where a quilt is layered with backing, batting, and top, then laid out on a large table and tied and knotted at even spaces with pearl cotton or yarn to hold it together instead of quilting it. High loft batting is usually used in tied quilts.

UFO

A term quilters use to refer to an unfinished quilt or project. Most quilters have many projects on the go at any one time.

UNFINISHED SIZE

The measurement of a block or quilt before the ¼" seam allowance is sewn.

For example, instructions may say

"Block size 10" finished, 10 ½" unfinished" This means, when you have finished the individual block it will be 10 ½" square before you sew it too another block. But when the quilt is complete, block will be 10" square.

UFO

Unfinished object - we all have lots!

WALKING FOOT

Presser foot attachment that helps to easily feed more than two layers at the same rate. It acts as an upper feed dog. The foot lifts in time with the feed dogs at each stitch. When it lowers to make the next stitch, the teeth catch the fabric and assist the lower feed dogs to pull the sandwich, or any thick fabric, through the machine.

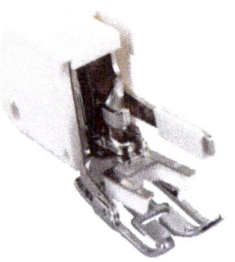

WIDTH OF FABRIC

Acronym - WOF

Width of fabric. You will find this abbreviation in many quilting patterns.

The width of your fabric is important. If the pattern calls for a strip that is WOF (the width of the fabric), it means 40" or 42 inches. Australian fabrics are usually 110cm wide which is approximately 43 cm. Australian quilters need to measure 42" and *not use the width of the fabric* or you will be way out in your quilting and your finished block will be wonky.

This is why quilting rulers are essential - they are marked in inches. **NEVER** *try to use a decimal ruler. It is disastrous.*

Common Quilting Acronyms

BOM: Block of the Month
BSK: Basic Sewing Kit
COB: Cut on the Bias
DSM: Domestic Sewing Machine
FD: Face Down
FMQ: Free Motion Quilting
FQ: Fat Quarter
FTF: Face to Face
FW: Feather Weight
HST: Half-Square Triangle

QAYG: Quilt As You Go
QST: Quarter-Square Triangle
RSD: Right Side Down
RST: Right Sides Together
SA: Seam Allowance
SID: Stitch in Ditch
SOG: Straight of Grain
STASH: Special Treasures All Secretly Hidden
TBQ: To Be Quilted

I'm working on my
PHD

in
Quilting

LAQ: Long Arm Quilting
LQS: Local Quilt Shop
MAQ: Mid-arm Quilting
OBW: One Block Wonder
PhD: Projects Half Done
PP: Paper Piecing
QAL: Quilt Along

TOT: Tone-on-Tone
UFO: Unfinished Object
WIP: Work in Progress
WISP: Work In Slow Progress
WOF: Width of Fabric
WST: Wrong Sides Together
BDNQ: Bad Day, Not Quilting

Funny Quilting Acronyms

FART: Fabric Accumulation Road Trip

FOB: Fear of Binding

HIPS: Hundreds of Ideas Piling Skyward

HSY: Haven't Started Yet

JRB: Jelly Roll Blues

PIGS: Projects in Grocery Sacks

ROOFS: Ran Out Of Fabric - Screaming!

SABLE: Stash Accumulation Beyond Life Expectancy

SEX: Stash Enhancing eXcursion

SQUID: Sewing a Quilt Until I Die

TGIF: Thank God It's Finished

TUS: The Usual Suspects

WBS: Wobbly Block Syndrome

WOMBAT: Waste of Money, Batting, and Time

WHIMM: Works Hidden In My Mind

WIWMI: Wish It Would Make Itself

WWIT: What was I thinking?

I suffer from

O C S D

Obsessive Compulsive Sewing Disorder

The best tools for a painless project

For Beginners- start with basic tools

If you are a senior or physically challenged, You have the advantage of being able to start the right way, with the right tools. Those of us who already have tools may need to replace our old faithfuls with one or two new, specialised pieces of equipment. You do not need every tool on the market for a successful quilt-making experience, but there are a few that are essential and some that will make a significant difference if you have physical challenges.

On the other hand, if you aren't yet sure that quilting is your thing, and you want to try it for a while before you commit to better tools, you can purchase a basic set in person or online from quilting stores or large chains such as Spotlight, Lincraft or Hobbysew. Beginning quilters need only to buy a basic beginner's set of tools - self-healing mat, ruler, rotary cutter, unpicker and pins. This is a typical inexpensive set. Just bear in mind that the cutter may not meet your needs if you have arthritis in your hand or if your shoulders are painful and stiff.

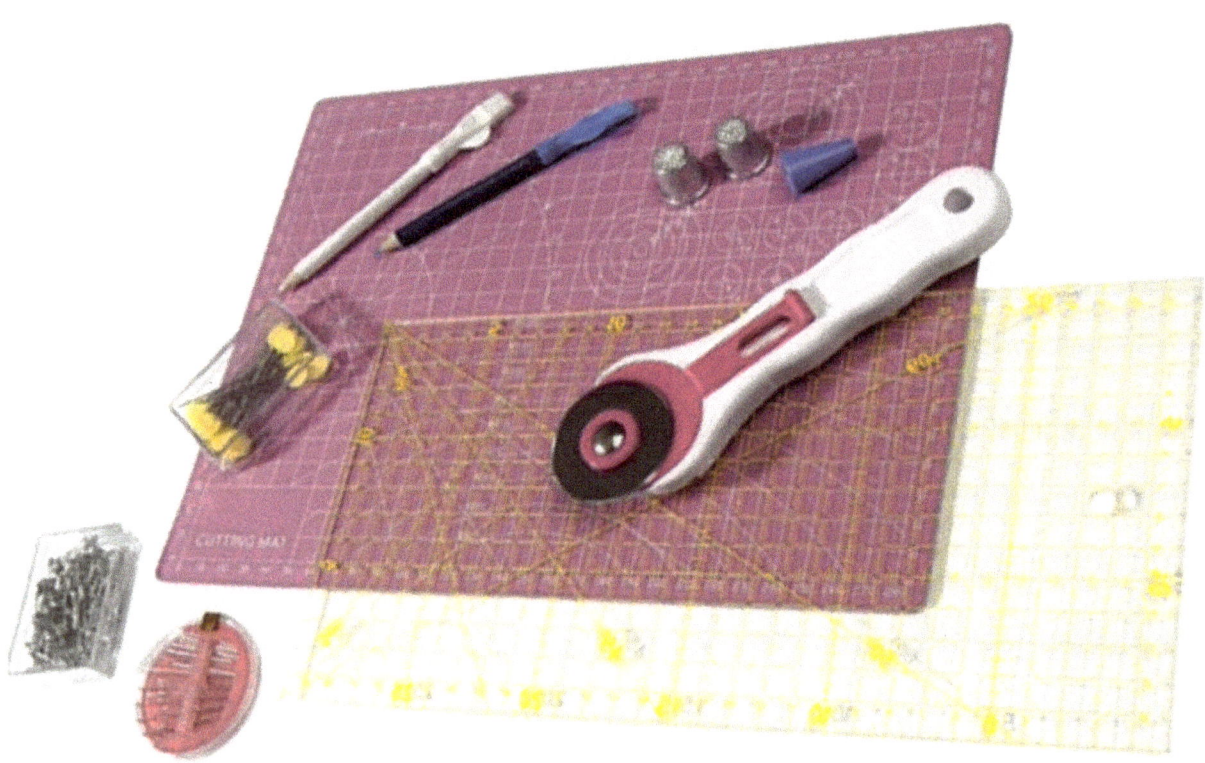

It's a good idea to make friends with your Local Quilt Shop (LQS).

Quilt shops also sell tools, as well as fabric, thread, patterns and other goods that are used for quilting. They often have group sewing and quilting classes where beginners and experienced can learn how to sew or quilt and how to use different advanced techniques.

Rotary Cutters for problem hands and wrists

This tool is a fabric "pizza cutter". The blades are very sharp and cut fabric quickly and accurately. You can use scissors but you will not get the accuracy quilting demands.

There are various brands and types of rotary cutter. Your choice will depend on what you can afford, but also on whether you have special needs that a particular cutter will meet. The golden rule is "You get what you pay for." Once you have decided that you are going to dive into quilting, it is time to buy high-quality cutters to meet your specific needs. Finding a quality cutter means you will have less cost in replacing blades, less waste of fabric and less wasted effort in cutting.

If you have problems with arthritis, carpel tunnel syndrome, tendonitis, hand fatigue, neck or arm pain, or if you are left handed, I recommend TrueCut's My Comfort Cutter*. It makes cutting easier and comes in left-handed or right-handed models. It pairs with the TrueCut rulers, providing a straight cut solution for quilters with stiff hands or tremors that make holding a cutter and keeping the cutter against a ruler's edge.

One is enough to start with. A good all purpose cutter is 45mm cutter. As you progress, you may find it easier for finer work to have a smaller cutter, and for large quilts, a 60mm rotary cutter will allow you to cut through up to 4 or 6 layers of fabric at the same time.

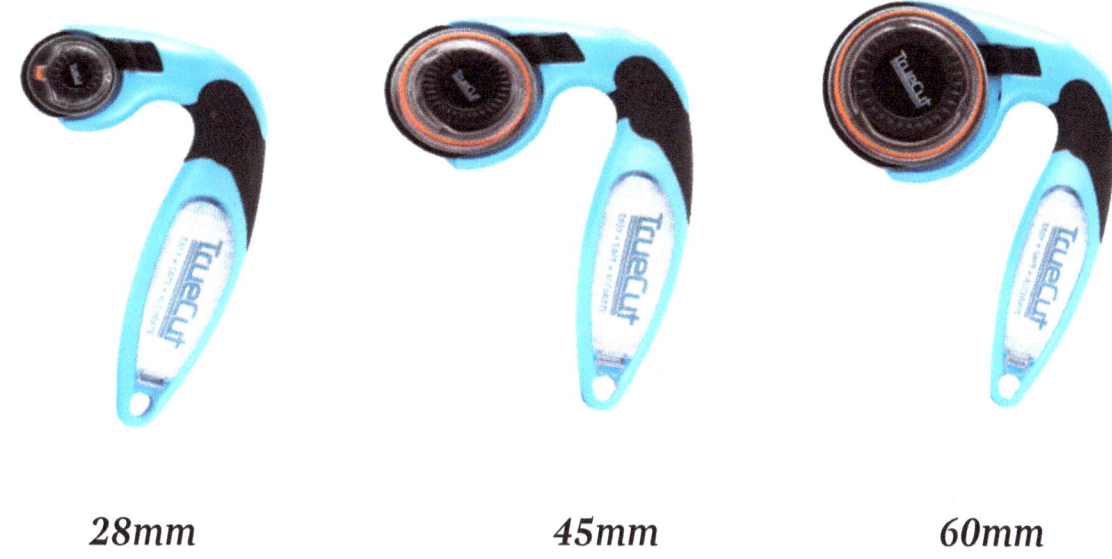

28mm   *45mm*   *60mm*

Care for your cutter

Like a carpenter takes care of his tools, keeping his chisels and saws clean and sharp, every quilter needs to take care of their rotary cutters.

Accuracy in cutting depends on having a good, sharp blade, which depends on how you treat it.

- Always close the blade when it not in use. If you drop the cutter and it's closed, the blade won't be damaged when it hits the floor. A chipped or dented blade is useless and has to be thrown away and replaced.

- Only ever cut fabric. Paper, plastic or wood will blunt the blade.

- Clean your blade after every cutting session. Carefully take the blade out of the cutter, remember it's very sharp. Use a soft cloth to clean the blade and the housing to remove any fluff or dust lodged between them. Then replace the blade, being sure to follow the instructions that came with your cutter.

- Change or, if your blade is the right kind, sharpen your blade after every quilt, or 15 hours of quilting, whichever comes first.

There are several kinds of blade sharpener. With some you sharpen by pushing the blade down a groove that has sharpening stones on either side. Others are electric, which means you take the blade out of the cutter, place it in the sharpener and follow the instruction as to how long and how often to run it for each side of the blade.

If you have a True Cut straight or Comfort Cutter, there are both kinds of blade sharpener for their blades and any other blade that can be sharpened. Both are easy to use, take just about any blade and do a great job.

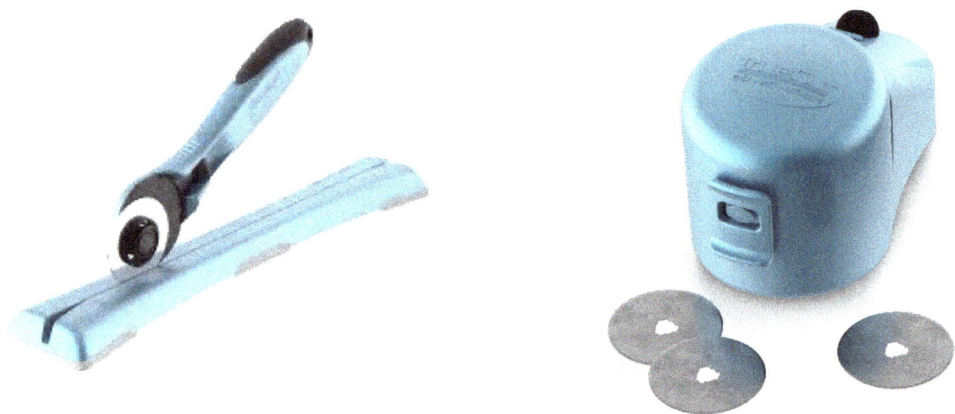

Of course, not all blades can be sharpened. Some are meant to be discarded as soon as they are worn out. If you discard blades, please do so safely.

You will find some suggestions of ways to discard damaged or worn sharps further on in the book.

Cutting mats

Self-healing Cutting Mat

This is an essential item. If you try to cut with a rotary cutter on a table, you WILL damage yourself, your cutter and the table.

A self-healing mat protects the cutting surface, fabric, and wheel and ensures accuracy. Any cuts in the surface heal themselves, preventing grooves that push your cutting wheel off track.

Most cutting mats have a ruler-grid printed on the surface that can also help with measuring fabric pieces. However, never measure using the mat grid. Always use a ruler. If you can, purchase a mat that has clear angle lines of 30 degrees, 45 degrees and 600. These are extremely helpful when you need to cut one or more sides of a shape at a different angle to its base. For example, a 600 degree triangle or a 450 trapezoid.

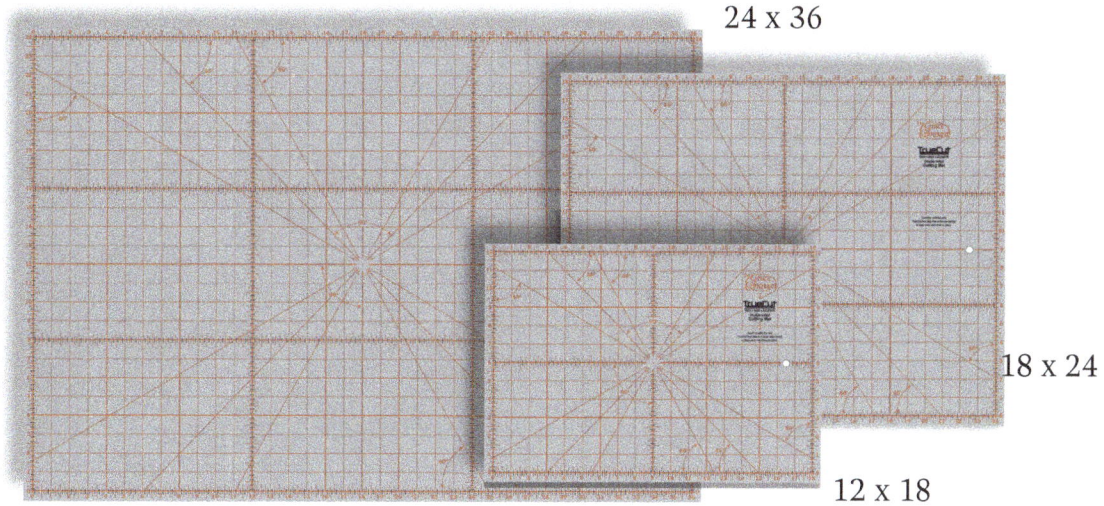

24 x 36

18 x 24

12 x 18

Mats come in various sizes, but for quilt-as-you-go, a large mat is unnecessary. An 18x24 inch mat is a good size to start with.

Mats range in price according to quality and brand. Choose the mat with;

- a background that makes the markings easy to read, especially through a ruler,
- the angles lines clearly marked,
- a good reputation for longevity, and
- a price within your budget.

Rotating cutting mat

There are some tools that make your life so much easier. This is one of them. Not only does it make your job easier and faster, but also more precise and neat. When cutting or aligning fabric, we quilters must constantly lift and rearrange the fabric for efficient cutting. Not if you have a rotating mat!

The rotating cutting mat lets you to turn your fabric without moving it and then cut through several layers of fabric without worrying that a layer has moved and one piece will be out of shape. It is ideal for squaring blocks.

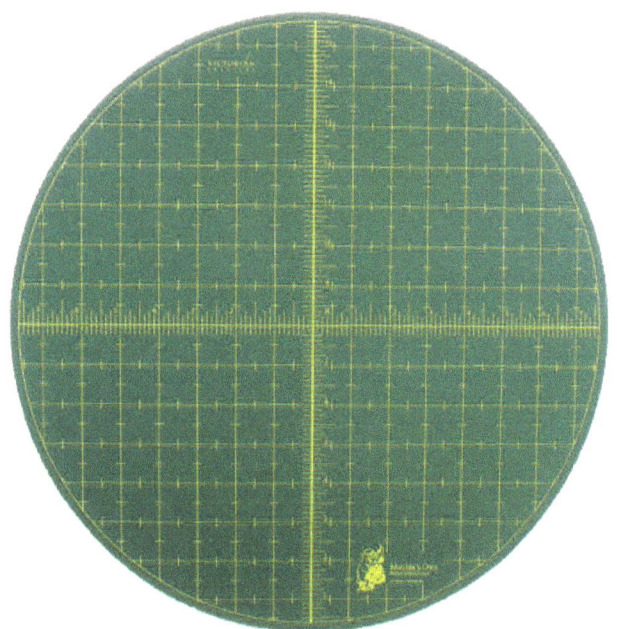

Rotating mats mostly come in 7", 12" and 15" and are round or square. Choose one that is self-healing. I recommend you buy a *square* mat that is at least 15 inches.

Why 15 inches? I have a 12" square mat, which I love. However, I sometimes find it is a little too small to square off a big block and I wish I had a 15" mat.

Why square? With a circle mat, the width is only at its maximum in the middle. A 15 inch block would hang over the edge of the 15" mat at the corners.

Turning a square mat on my cutting table takes more room to turn due to its corners, but the advantage is that you have the full 15 inches to work on from top to bottom.

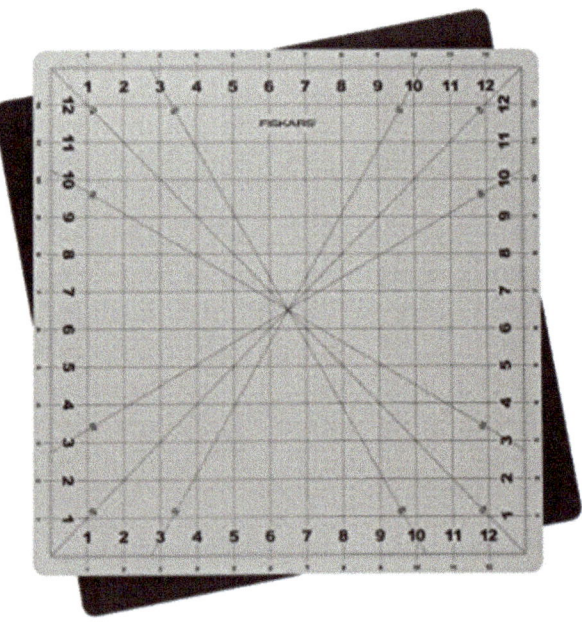

Rulers

Quilting rulers are an essential tool. You will only cut your pieces quickly and accurately if you use an accurate quilting ruler. The thickness and straight edge of the quilting ruler determine your safety. Using a rotary cutter with a wooden ruler is dangerous. There are many shapes and sizes of ruler;

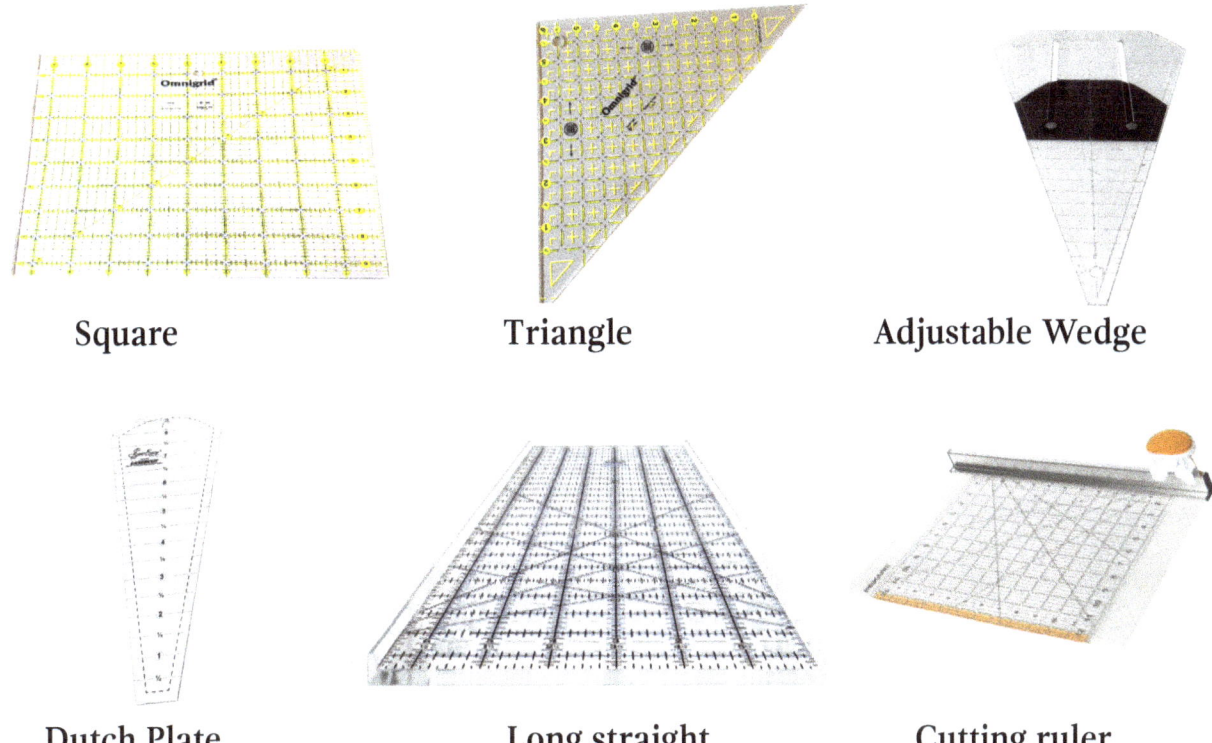

Square   Triangle   Adjustable Wedge

Dutch Plate   Long straight   Cutting ruler

There are other rulers, some of which are either nice-to-haves or a waste of money. You really only need a few basic rulers.

The must haves are;

- A large (15 ½ inch) medium (6 ½ inch) and small (4 ½ inch) square ruler
- A long straight ruler (at least 15 inch long and 6 ½ inches wide)

If you buy a beginners set of quilting tools there will be a straight ruler included. Once you are sure you are going to stick with quilting, you will find a square ruler the most useful one to add to your kit.

I suggest starting with a 15 ½-inch square ruler. This allows you to cut accurately across folded and single thickness fabric, square off your blocks and see the measurements on the ruler clearly.

Later, when you can afford it, get a long ruler with a built in rotary cutter. This is invaluable for cutting your batting, which is a thicker, wider non-woven fabric.

Rulers for senior hands

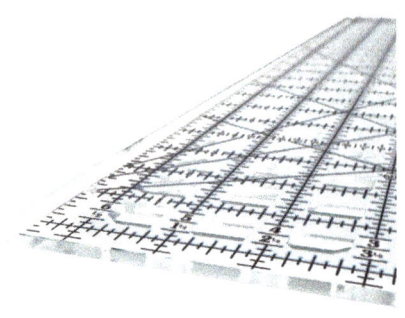

Cutter Guide / Ruler Track

For those of us who have problem hands, such as a tremor, weakness or painful arthritis, there is a set of rulers that I find a godsend.

TrueCut has developed a ruler that solves one of our most common cutting frustrations, slipping and veering away from the ruler's edge. The track and guide rulers paired with a Comfort Cutter prevents slipping and keeps all of your cuts straight and true. The rulers have a raised edge, or track, on both sides, and in the case of square rulers, all around. The ruler's edge adds more surface area for the rotary blade to rest against. This gives a safer and more stable cut, while preventing the cutter from skipping onto the ruler.

The edge doesn't take any extra space or add to your measurements. The rulers have built in holes, which allow your fingers to press onto both the fabric and the ruler to keep them steady as you cut.

The Comfort Cutter's best feature is the removable guide. It slips over the raised edge of the ruler, the ruler track, ensuring that the rotary blade always remains against the ruler's edge. The guide can be removed quickly and easily to allow you to use with other rulers.

Any quilter who has the slightest hand tremor can be sure that with care they will cut a straight line!

Caring for your rulers

Keep your rulers clean, using a cool damp cloth or spectacles cleaner cloth. Any scratches, cuts or chips along the edge or corners of your ruler cause the cutter blade to go off track. Correct cutting prevents damage. Most square ruler corner chips come from dropping it, or knocking the corner on a hard object. Never leave your rulers - or cutting mats - on a table or in a car in the hot sun. They *will* warp. Keep them cool and flat. Most rulers have a small hole at the top of the ruler. This allows you to hang the ruler on a hook, safely out of the way, and in a position that will keep it straight and flat. There are stands available for rulers, but they take up bench or table space.

Unless you are hand quilting, you need access to a sewing machine. You don't need a fancy embroidery or quilting machine. Your machine only needs to be reliable and of reasonable quality, and you must have good access to service and spare parts. All your machine needs to do is a straight stitch and possibly a little zigzag. Your old faithful will do the job!

Scissors and other essential cutters

Scissors

If we use rotary cutters to cut out all of our shapes, why do we need scissors? The simple answer answer if that rotary cutters don't do everything. There will be times when you decide to use a single piece of fabric for you backing, rather than backing each block as you quilt as you go. You may need to trim all the way down the side of a quit and that can be hard to do with a cutter.

Rotary cutters are not good for snipping threads, and it's easier to snip the tails off a small seam with a pair of scissors while you are at the machine than getting up to go to the cutting mat.

If you are using fabric that frays easily, pinking shears can be a blessing to trim the selvedge before you before you start cutting.

There are so many different brands and kinds of scissors, which do we need, and which are the best for us? When shopping for scissors, these factors are of the utmost importance;

- quality blade
- hand comfort
- fitness for purpose

Good tools give good results. Yes, you will pay for quality, but they are a lifetime tool, provided you choose stainless steel blades and comfortable handles. Carbon steel will rust, stainless steel will not. Having a nice pair of scissors for small cuts and a high-quality pair of shears helps you attain better results for your project.

The primary purpose of scissors in quilting is cutting long lengths of fabric. Shears are the best tool for this. They have bent handles that shift the hand slightly up from the blades. The thumb loop is smaller than the loop where the fingers enter. This design allows the fabric to stay flat while you work the blades. However, some shears are heavy and quickly tire the hand and wrist. Blades over 10 inches can be awkward to manipulate if you have arthritis in your hands. The good news is there's a solution. Fiskars have produces spring loaded scissors that can also fill the role of both shears and scissors, their No.8 Premier Easy Action Bent Scissors. If arthritis is making your quilting activities painful, the spring mechanism, which opens the blades after each cut, spares you hand fatigue and pain. The Arthritis Foundation recommends this product for people who have lost hand strength or struggle with arthritis pain. The blades are stainless steel and the handles are cushioned. It can be used by both right and left handed users and is less expensive that many other high quality shears.

Scissors are a shorter tool. They usually have symmetrical handles, with both loops being the same size. Small sewing scissors, for example, may only be about 4 to 5 inches long. Their short blades are meant for snipping threads instead of cutting fabric.

Quilter who like to use appliqués on there project need small scissors to cut around the appliqué shapes, getting right into tiny corners and tight curves. There is a scissor perfect for this purpose, as well as for snipping threads, that comes in a range of sizes.

The Karen Kay Buckley serrated edge scissors makes is appliqué easy, as the blade prevents the tiniest pieces of fabric from moving during the cutting process.

They come in a range of sizes right down to a tiny 4". They have stainless steel blades and are suitable for both left and right handed users. Karen Kay Buckley also produce a small multi-purpose scissors, with a curved blade ideal for snipping threads while free motion or controlled quilting the piece on the machine.

Caring for your shears and scissors

The number one rule for caring for your quilting scissors and shears is never use them to cut anything else but fabric. I have a sign on my quilting room wall -

"You touch-a my scissors, I cut off-a your hands!"

The second rule is, if you have a blade shield supplied with the scissors/shears, use it. It will protect the blades from damage if they are dropped or fall on a hard surface and from moisture. This is particularly important if the blades are carbon steel.

If your scissors/shears have started to dull, you can have them sharpened by a specialist knife sharpener, or you may obtain a scissors sharpening tool and sharpen them yourself.

Do not try to sharpen them with a domestic knife sharpener. They are sharpened in a different configuration that kitchen knives.

Seam Ripper – no shame here!

Even the best of quilters/seamstresses stand by their seam ripper. Because I use them so often, I have at least 2 located strategically throughout the house. It's almost impossible to complete a sewing project without using a seam ripper (also known as a stitch ripper, unpicker, or stitch unpicker). They are absolutely essential for pulling out mistake stitches.

There are a lot of different styles of seam ripper. There are tiny ones that come with your sewing machine, short ones, long ones and ergonomic seam ripper s, one with a special "seam eraser" and another seam ripper with a magnifier and light, which is good for people with bad eyesight. There's even a fancy brass one in a shiny brass case.

Any seam ripper will work, but for those of us with hand problems, do yourself a huge favour and buy an ergonomic ripper with a wide, non-slip handle. All seam rippers have the same main structure: a handle with a metal tip. The tip has a blade between a point and a little red ball. That little ball lets you rip out stitches very quickly.

So many quilters spend hours picking painstakingly at each stitch in a seam on the wrong side of the fabric.

Here's the correct way to unpick.

1. Working on the **right** side of the fabric, gently pull on the fabric until you can see the stitches.

2. Stick the pointed tip under a stitch that needs to be removed. The first stitch is always the hardest one to pick out, so take care to catch only the thread. Don't poke it through the fabric.

3. Push the seam ripper gently so that the stitch slides to the blade in the curve and then push a little more so that the blade cuts through the thread . Keep going until the stitches that need to be removed are gone.

But what if you have a long seam to unpick? Here is the way to go about unpicking it.

1. Insert the ball between the two layers of fabric with the blade against the stitches.

2. Hold the fabric with your left hand and the seam ripper with your right (or vice versa if you are a leftie).

3. Pull the fabric a little towards you (or just hold it still) while you push the seam ripper a little away from you (in the direction of the arrow above and to the left

4. The blade will cut right through the whole line of stitches, gathering them up. The ball slides easily against the fabric without cutting or poking into it.

You will find that using the seam ripper correctly will mean less time unpicking and more time doing what you most enjoy!

Fabric cutting machines

If you have serious arthritis or hand strength issues, and cutting is too painful or difficult to contemplate, you may want to consider an electronic fabric cutter. There are many types and brands on the market but all of them have the same purpose, to cut out the pieces of fabric you need to make your quilt. Any of these machines is a financial investment, but it is well worth the money if it keeps you able to quilt.

While there are two different modes of operation, manual and digital, fabric cutting machines have two things in common;

- They cut the shape of your fabric pieces and
- They are highly accurate.

Manual Machines

A manual cutting machine requires manual operation. Fabric is placed between a die (stamp) which determines the shapes to be cut, and a mat that holds the fabric. You turn the handle, which puts them through the cutting machine.

Users agree that a manual machine offers many advantages;

- more precise and accurate cuts than a rotary blade
- a safer way to cut. You are not physically handling the blade.
- few moving parts, so they tend to last longer than electronic machines
- no power source needed
- cheaper to run
- can be used anywhere
- highly portable, easy to pack up the machine and take it on the go.

Digital Machines

Digital machines are the simplest way to cut through fabric if you have arthritis or any other difficulty in using manual machines. They work in a very different way to manual. There are no dies. The machine The machine takes the information from the design and cuts each curve and line as the fabric passes through the machine.

Digital machines offer many advantages;

- unlimited design options
- no dies to store, and
- you can upload your own designs for free.

It would be natural to assume that digital machines are faster than manuals, but this isn't always the case. Compared to a manual machine, it may take longer for a digital machine to trace out the shape and design and cut the fabric.

Choosing a machine

There are a number of things you need to consider before you decide to make what is a sizeable financial commitment.

1. **Size of the Machine** - Some machines are larger or more compact than others. Anytime you bring a new tool into your crafting room, you have to consider your space and how much of it you can spare. Usually manual machines are smaller and more portable, about the size of a toaster. You can store them anywhere, and you can use them anywhere. Electronic cutting machines have a design very similar to a computer printer. If you're short on space or interested in portability, then a manual machine may be a good option for you.

2. **Accuracy of cutting fabric** - With the exception of a few brands and models, most fabric cutting machines are designed to cut paper and similar materials. Many models can't cut all types of fabrics, or you may be limited to how many layers you can cut at one time. Consider your needs. What types of fabric do you usually cut? How often will you need to use the machine? How many layers do you need to cut at one time?
Customer reviews may also give you some insight into the model's fabric-cutting capabilities.

3. **Included Accessories** - Most fabric cutting machines come with accessories that will help you get started. When comparing machines, keep these accessories in mind. Manual machines will typically come with starter mats and dies. Electric cutting machines may come with mats and built-in designs that you can start using right away. Some machines will also come with pattern books. Make sure that the machine at least includes everything you need to get started. If you already have a collection of dies, make sure that they will be compatible with your new machine.

4. **Price** - This will be a consideration when choosing a cutting machine. In fact, price will probably be a deciding factor for most people. Before you even start looking at and comparing machines, set your budget. How much can you comfortably spend? Once you have a budget, you can start looking at machines in your price range. Don't be tempted to buy the cheapest machine you can find, it's worth spending more for a quality, durable machine.

5. **Versatility** - It may not be the first thing you thin of when comparing cutting machines. But what else can the machine do? Can it be used for other crafts? The machines – both manual and digital – can be used to make paper crafts, stickers and a variety of other crafts.
Electronic machines may offer more versatility because you can use different attachments for different functions. Once you have a machine with such options you may find new, fun ways to create.

6. **Ease of Use** - This is one of the most important considerations when choosing a cutting machine. If it's too complicated, you'll probably never use it. Read the product description and reviews. Electronic machines may be more complex, but can be more user-friendly designs than others. Manual machines are usually the easiest to use. They don't have any electronic functions. Simply stack the die, fabric and mat properly, and then run it through the machine.

If you believe that a cutting machine will allow you to keep on quilting longer, and if you are prepared and able to make the financial commitment, here are some machines that are available in Australia, as well as the US and UK.

Manual

The AccuQuilt Ready. Set. GO! is designed especially for quilters. If you're new to die cutting, it may be a great option for you. It includes everything you need to get started with fabric cutting, including:

- Qube 8″ Mix & Match Block
- The fabric cutting machine
- Strip Cutter 2½″
- Two cutting mats: 10″ x 24″ and 6″ x 6″
- Die pick
- Qube book written by Eleanor burns
- More than 70 free patterns

Accuquilt Go! Fabric Cutter can cut large pieces of fabric. You can cut up to six layers of fabric at one time, and the design of this machine minimises arm strain. It can cut up to six layers of fabric at once, is lightweight and easy to use. However, there's not a lot included in the package, certainly not a lot of dies.

It comes with;

- the machine
- the Value Die, 6" x 12" cutting mat,
- a 20-page pattern booklet,
- and a die pick

Sizzix Big Shot - more of a paper crafters machine than a quilters. It comes with;

- One Extended Multi Purpose Platform
- One pair of Standard Cutting Pads.
- One year limited warranty

I would have my doubts that this would be fit for purpose for quilting.

Digital

Brother ScanNCut SDX1250 This machine, one of the latest ScanNCut models, is a stand alone and does not require a computer. It has scanning capability, enabling you to scan and cut your own patterns. It is well know as being an excellent fabric cutter, with all the advantages of a general cutter as well.

It comes with

- Auto Blade Holder and Blade
- Rotary Auto Blade Kit
- Standard Mat 12 x 12 inches
- Low Tack Mat 12 x 12 inch
- My Connection Activation Card: Transfer your designs back and forth between the ScanNCut SDX1250 and the Brother XP plus the following accessories
    - Pen Holder, Water Erase Pen, Air Erase Pen, High Tack Support Sheet (4), Touch Pen, Spatula, Accessory Pouch

Cricut Explorer 3 Cricut comes in two models, the Maker 3 and the Explorer 3. Only the Explorer 3 lists fabric as one of the materials it can cut.

Cricut was originally designed to meet the needs of the paper craft creator. Cards, banners, home decor and labels.

While the Explorer 3 can cut fabric, I have not yet see any reviews from quilters and sewers as to its ability to meet their needs.

Sizzix Big Shot Switch is the electronic version of the Big Shot but seems to be solely focussed on paper crafts. It is not a digital version and relies on dies for its cutting.

It's a big investment. My advice is to thoroughly test drive any manual or digital cutter that you might consider purchasing. The Craft and Quilting shows, Craft Alive, and other such events give you the opportunity to take classes and see live demonstrations of their capability.

Sewing machines

If you don't have a sewing machine, invest in one of a reputable brand. Your machine will be your quilting workhorse for many years, it has to be up for the job.

Get to know your machine

Your sewing machine manual is your best friend. Modern machines often have a digital manual. It's worth the trouble to download and print it. Keep it by your machine - use it!

Get to know how to use these parts of your machine.

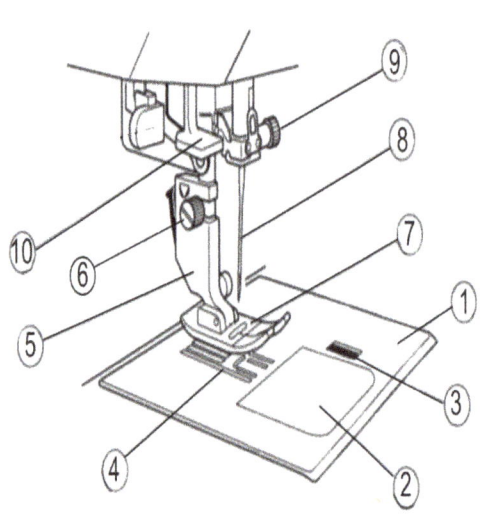

1. **Needle plate** - this covers the moving parts around the needle and bobbin areas. You will need to remove this to clean the bobbin and sewing areas of lint and dust.

2. **Bobbin cover** - take this cover off to change your bobbins. Your sewing machine manual will tell you how to place your bobbin and thread the lower cotton.

3. **Bobbin cover release** - Your machine may have a release to flip open the cover. Check your manual.

4. **Feed dogs** - the little teeth on your sewing machine that feed your fabric evenly through the machine. They produce perfectly spaced, even stitches. To free motion quilt, drop the feed dogs below the needle plate. This allows you to manually move your quilt. Attempting to free motion quilt with the feed dogs up results in broken needles.

Your machine's manual will show you how to drop the feed dogs. If you have an older machine, you may not be able to drop the feed dogs. There may be a metal plate supplied to cover the feed dogs instead. Again, check your manual.

5. **Presser foot holder** - This holds the presser foot that smoothes and flattens the fabric as it is fed through the machine and stitched. If you want to change to another presser foot;

    - Use the release lever to drop off the foot. (Check your manual for where it is and how to use it.)
    - Raise the foot holder and press the foot release lever to drop the foot.
    - Put it in the accessories box so you don't misplace it.
    - Place the next foot below the holder, lower the foot holder, which then clicks onto the new foot.

6. **Accessories attachment screw** - If you want to change from an ordinary presser foot to a walking foot, you need to unscrew the presser foot holder and replace it with the walking foot. If you are going to free motion quilt you will need to remove the presser foot holder and replace it with the free motion quilting accessories.
Check your manual for instructions.

7. **Presser foot** - You may have a wide range of specialised presser feet supplied with your machine for various purposes.. Your manual should have instructions on how to use each of them and how to fit them to your machine.
There is a setting on most machines that allows you to adjust the amount of pressure that is on the presser foot. Every brand and model of machine seems to be different in how this is achieved. Again, check your manual.
If you can't find a presser foot pressure adjustment, you may not be able to lower the pressure for Controlled Quilting (More on this quilting method later).

8. **Needle**

9. **Needle clamp screw** - Release the screw to remove the old needle and replace it with the new.

    - One side of the needle will be flat. When you slide a new needle into position, make sure that the flat side of the needle is against the flat side of the clamp.
    - Slide it all the way up and and then firmly tighten the clamp screw.

10. **Needle threader** - different sewing machine brands and models have different kinds of needle threaders. On the diagram, the machine's needle threader is to the side of the needle and pulls down, others are are below the needle plate. Some are easy to use, others are not. It's often quicker and easier to manually thread the needle.
A great hint from one of my quilting class members is to hold a white bread tag or a piece of white card behind the eye of the needle. It makes it easier to see the hole.

Accessories

To make quilting easier and more accurate there are two accessories you will need, the ¼ inch foot to make your seams exactly the right width and the walking foot to make it easy to sew through the thickness of the sandwich evenly. Your sewing machine shop will have these to fit your sewing machine, or you may find a universal model that will fit any machine.

¼ inch foot   Universal Walking foot

Care for your machine

Your sewing machine is your workhorse. Treat it with respect and tender care. If you do, it will give you good service for many years.

- Keep your machine covered and protected from dust when not in use.

- After you finish a quilt, remove the needle plate and throughly clean the lint from around the bobbin and inside the bobbin holder. If you have a small lint brush supplied with your machine, use that, if not a medium soft paintbrush is great. At the same time, change the needle. Needles lose their sharp tip over long periods of use.

- Turn off and unplug your sewing machine when you are away from it. Sewing machines can generate considerable heat when left on, and a lightning strike when a sewing machine is plugged in can cause irreversible damage.

- Have your machine serviced regularly by a technician familiar with your model. Sewing machines can last many years when they are kept in good working order by a reliable and skilled mechanic.

My very first machine, a gift from my beloved Nanny Leah in the 1950s, was a Singer treadle machine. It had been hers from the 1920s. There are quilters who still use the old treadle and hand operated sewing machines to quilt. Like us, ageing sewing machines in good order are not too old to create beautiful quilts.

In 2017, I upgraded to the Janome Horizon 8900 from my previous sewing machine, also a Janome, which was then over 30 years old. It went to a new home and is still going strong.

Why did I upgrade?

Certainly not because the old Janome was on its last legs, it wasn't, but I knew that the new model would give me the ability to do more quilting, with less effort, for much longer. It had;

- a wider throat, making manipulating the quilt through the machine as I quilted much easier on my back, which is ageing and arthritic.
- a stitch regulator I can use when I'm too sore to press the foot pedal. All I have to do is flip out the pedal chord, set the stitch speed and push the Start/Stop button to sew or stop sewing.
- it is future proof; the right tool for my body then, now and into the future.

Eight years on I love my new sewing machine. It's my best friend in my happy place. Later on, if you want to have better functions to help you to keep sewing, or do more complex quilting, you too might consider upgrading your machine. That's the beauty of quilting. You can choose your tools to suit your needs, your ambition, and your pocket.

Upgrading your machine

If and when it comes time to upgrade your machine, and BEFORE you go near the shops or searching online;

- Set a budget and stick to it no matter what.
- Make a list of all the things you would like your new machine to do for you that aren't possible with your current machine. For example, you want to free-motion quilt and your current machine won't allow you to drop the feed dogs, or you want to try Controlled Motion quilting and you can't lower the foot pressure.
- Rank your needs in priority order and separate the needs from the nice-to-haves in case you have to compromise because of price.
- Ask your quilting friends what machines they have, what its features are and how reliable and easy to use it is.
- Ask them if you can test drive their machine to see if it suits you.

Once you decide on a brand and model, there's research to be done.

- Do some price comparisons with different dealers and distributors.
- Find a supplier with a good reputation for reliable service and maintenance, and *reasonable prices.*
- Ask people who have that machinecwhere they purchased it and what back up service and assistance they received.
  If someone had a bad experience, they will be only too happy to tell you!

Once you have a good idea of what you intend to buy, visit some dealers.

- Make sure you tell the dealer that you want the machine for quilting and that you would like one with a wide throat and with quilting accessories included. (The throat is the space between the right side where the controls are and the needle. The wider the space between these, the easier it is to move the quilt or block through the machine when quilting.)

- Show that you have done your price comparisons and ask the best price, or at least a price match. Don't be afraid to walk away and find a good deal. However, if a dealer gives better service, or offers some free add-ons, such as an extension table, or extra accessories, it may be worth paying that little more.

- Above all - choose the machine with which you are comfortable;
    - comfortable with its features,
    - comfortable sewing on it,
    - comfortable that the price fits within your budget.

Whatever you do, take the lessons that are offered by dealer. They will save you hours of poring over the manual, not to mention broken needles and wasted fabric caused by such simple mistakes as wrongly threading the machine.

When you have your new machine, enjoy it! Give it a name and talk to it. It's going to be your companion in your happy place for a long, long time.

Ironing is essential for accurate cutting. No matter what the temptation to skip this step, and believe me, I hate ironing with a passion, it's an absolute must. JUST DO IT!!!

Irons and ironing boards

Always, always iron before you cut. If you don't, you will regret it. It only takes one tiny wrinkle under that cutting wheel to put your block out of line. Before worrying about the best iron for the job, you need to think about what you will do with it.

Ironing and pressing are two different things.

Ironing is when you move an iron back and forth over fabric to smooth it out. You need to keep the movements constant so the fabric doesn't scorch. Before cutting and sewing fabric, iron it.

Pressing is lifting and setting your iron down. There is no back and forward movement on the fabric at all. Some pattern instructions are specific about this. If it says 'press', then press.

Once you've sewn a seam, joined two pieces of fabric together, press the seam.

1. Take the work to your ironing board, place it right side up and press your iron directly on top of the seam you have just sewn. Don't move the iron around.

2. After a few seconds, lift your iron. Continue pressing until the length of the seam is pressed. This gives you flatter seams and sets the stitches into the fabric.

3. Then turn the piece over and use your fingers or the tip of your iron to open the seam. This is the point at which fabric may stretch, so be careful.

4. When your seam is open, press it again.

What's important about irons?

1. **The Cord.** Before buying an iron, look at the cord. There are cords made specifically for left or right-handed users, and also irons that offer retractable cords, which is a great idea!

2. **The Weight.** Usually we like light, portable products, however a heavy iron helps to add some strength to pressing. If, like me your hands can't cope with that weight, choose one that has all the other features of a good iron and yet still is manageable for your physical ability. Check out the small quilting irons that are now on the market.

Steam

I never use water in my iron for quilting. Steam irons have a habit of squirting water which can affect the fabric. If I need a some water to deal with a stubborn wrinkle, I use a slightly damp cloth placed between the iron and the fabric or a fine mist spray bottle. I don't need a steam iron, which means I can choose the least expensive iron to meet my needs.

Price

Irons come in all shapes and sizes and prices. I have limited space in my happy place, and getting up and down to get to the ironing board is painful. I have a small iron and a board next to my sewing machine, just big enough to take a 12" block. That way I only have to get up to iron when I'm joining blocks and assembling a larger quilt. My small iron has no steam, is heavier that most mini irons but not too heavy for me to handle, plus it only cost me AU$18 on special at my local Spotlight store and I love it!!!

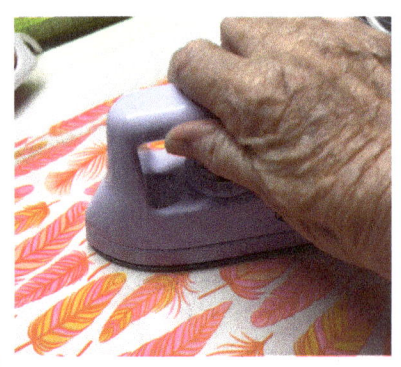

Highly popular amongst quilters are the Oliso Pro Plus, and the Rowenta, which retail at between AU$150 and AU$250 and three mini irons, with or without steam range from AU$25 - AU$125.

However, your current steam iron, without water, will do a good job for you. Your budget and common sense will guide you.

Ironing Boards

Ironing fabric and pressing seams is different to ironing clothes. Attempting to press a row of four 15 ½" blocks with a narrow ironing board can be a struggle. If you don't already have one, invest in an extra wide ironing board.

In Australia, Sunbeam make an Extra Large Chic ironing board which is 45cm wide, compared to the average 38cm'. However, you only need a large ironing board when you are assembling a large quilt. Most of the time you will press seams less than 20 inches long, which is why I have a mini board next to my sewing machine. I made it myself, so easily.

Make your own mini-ironing board (or get someone to make it for you.)

You will need;

- An old wooden cutting board or a piece of 90mm MDF about 300mm square.
- 1 piece of plain colour canvas (doesn't scorch) - 6 cm wider than the board .
- 2 pieces of batting - 4 cm larger than the board.
- 1 piece of non-skid mat - 2 cm smaller than the finished board.

Method

1. Place the canvas on a workbench, lay the batting on top of the canvas. There should be an even 2 cm of canvas showing around the batting.

2. Centre the board on the batting.

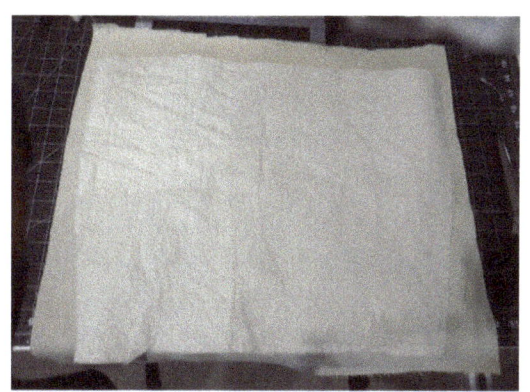

3. Choose one corner of the board and fold over the layers to cover that corner.

4. Staple the layers at the point of the triangle.

5. Without moving the board or layers, do the same at the opposite corner, stretching the layers tightly.

6. Repeat for the other two corners.

7. Fold the layers over the sides of the board, working on opposite sides, stretching the fabric tightly over the board.

8. Staple it down. Make sure that the gaps between staples are narrow.

9. Take the piece of non-skid matting and glue it to the bottom of the board, covering the staples.

Voila!
You have a mini-ironing board.

In conclusion

A visit to a craft fair or a Google search of quilting tools confirms how many companies are vying for our dollars. Quilters are a lucrative market for manufacturers.

When I first started out on my quilting journey the volume of enticing goodies to make quilting "more creative" was overwhelming. I have at least eight "fancy" rulers/templates that I have used once and then put away. I can count on one hand the number of tools that I use. I have six cutters, but I only use two. I have 7 different shaped rulers, of which I only use 3 constantly. I have a large mat and two rotating mats which are in constant use.

The message? **You don't need all the bits and pieces that you see at a Craft and Quilting fair.** There are some essential tools for quilters just setting out, and some great replacements for old hands who now need to consider some of the great ergonomic tools that are new to the market.

These are my suggested shopping lists. The first is the one I wish I had used when I wanted to start quilting and had no tools at all. The second is the list I had when I found out what was available for an old chook like me, with a bad back, a horrible hip and stiff hands, to make my work more comfortable and my quilting life longer.

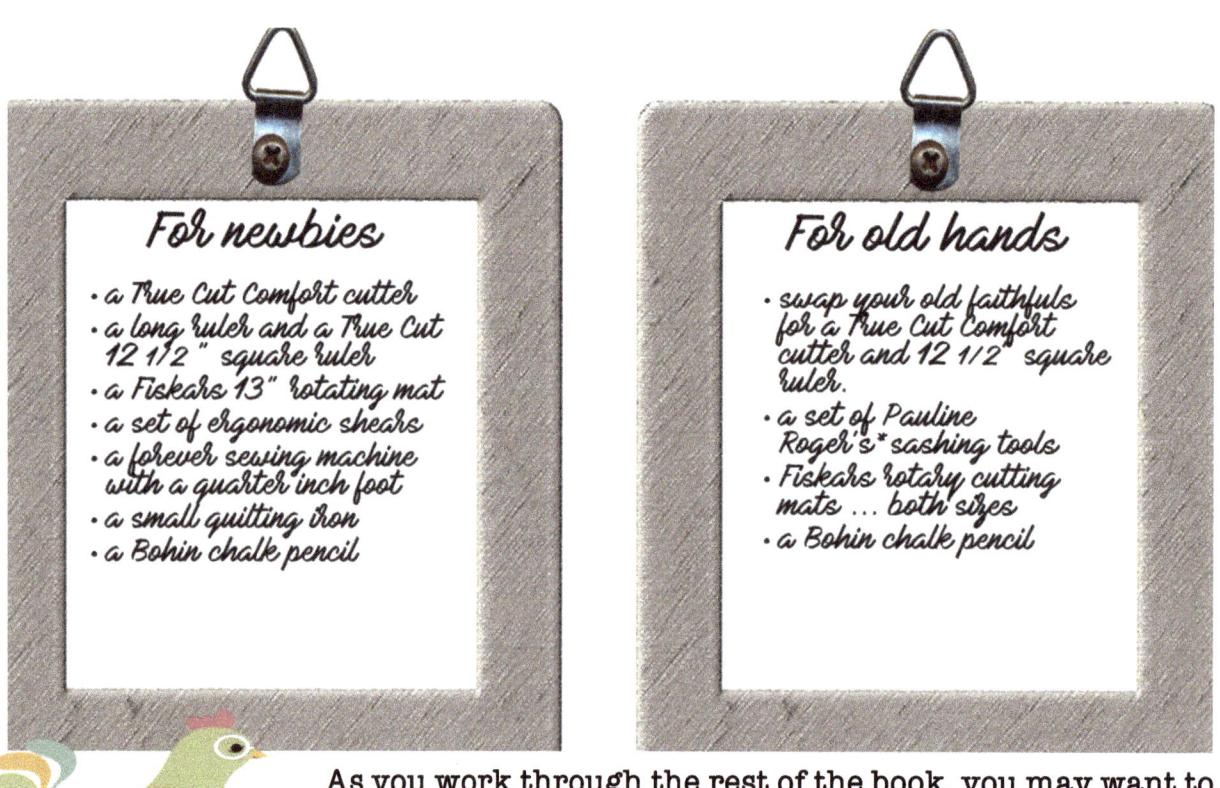

For newbies
- a True Cut Comfort cutter
- a long ruler and a True Cut 12 1/2" square ruler
- a Fiskars 13" rotating mat
- a set of ergonomic shears
- a forever sewing machine with a quarter inch foot
- a small quilting iron
- a Bohin chalk pencil

For old hands
- swap your old faithfuls for a True Cut Comfort cutter and 12 1/2" square ruler.
- a set of Pauline Roger's* sashing tools
- Fiskars rotary cutting mats ... both sizes
- a Bohin chalk pencil

As you work through the rest of the book, you may want to add some of the suggested special purpose tools to your list.
Never feel guilty.
We Old Chook Quilters have earned them.

Be it ever so humble...
It's Your Happy Place

Room to quilt and sew

Whenever I pick up a quilting book or magazine or watch a quilting video the surroundings look so salubrious! So clean and brand new! Social media is full of photographs of smart, well organised rooms, with neat and tidy fabric shelves, racks for cotton reels and sewing cabinets that do everything but the sewing for you.

Well, my sewing room is NOT like that, and never will be!!!! I don't have a bespoke quilting studio. My happy place is at best tidy, and at worst, chaotic. But then, I like it like that. I believe out of chaos comes something beautiful.

Your sewing space is your happy place it should be however and wherever you are comfortable to work, and whatever your budget will allow. If that's the kitchen table, and you are happy there, that's okay. If it's a guest bedroom that isn't often used as such, that's great!

New quilters often ask me whether they need a dedicated sewing room and what furniture they need to have. I ask them to ask themselves;

1. How big is your house? Are there enough rooms for everyone plus one that can be a dedicated sewing room? If not, is there somewhere you can set up a permanent area for sewing? Sometimes a verandah, a sunroom, an unused office or a store room can be converted. If there is enough outdoor space, and the budget to afford it, a "tiny house", converted garage or shed may do the trick.

2. How many people live in your house?

    - If you live by yourself, all you have to consider is what makes you happy and comfortable when you are sewing and quilting. You can do whatever you like.

    - If your household is two people, you need to discuss the possibilities with the other person. With a bit of negotiating you can work it out.

    - However, if you are a household of more than two you need to consider everyone's needs, activities and use of space. This can be challenging.

3. Are you strong enough to move and/or lift your sewing machine? If not, it is essential that you have an area where you can leave you machine permanently set up. You will need a table or cabinet which can be moved, with a gas lift to raise the machine whenever you need to sew.

Once you think you have the answers to these questions, discuss them with other people in the home, and work out what is possible for and achievable, then you can start to plan what furniture you need in your quilting space to will make it your "Happy Place".

What do you need in a quilting space?

There are six essentials;

- **Light** - quilting requires good vision. If the room is dark or casts shadows, you will need sources of good light to enable you to see your stitches. Consider lighting options.

- **Air** - a stuffy room is not a happy place. Not only do you need fresh air to be comfortable, you also need to be warm in winter and cool in summer. Hot summers mean perspiration and perspiration dripping on fabrics or sweaty hands handling them create stains. Consider the airflow.

- **Space** - Quilting is possible in small spaces. You need room for a table for your machine and a chair. Cutting is possible on a dining table or breakfast bar. Think about how you can utilise the space you have.

- **Quiet** - quilting requires high levels of focus. A busy room, with people traffic, telephone conversations and constant interruption, does not make for good concentration. If you are using common family areas, choose your quilting times for when you know the house is quiet, others are at work, or out shopping, playing or exercising.

- **Furniture** - There is no need to purchase expensive quilting furniture if there are items already in your home that you can commandeer. However, this has its down-side. If you commandeer the dining table as a machine table, you may have to pack up each day for breakfast, lunch and dinner. The breakfast bar is the best of cutting tables. It has the right height for standing to cut, and a firm surface for your cutting mat. Rotary cutting is not usually an overnight task.

- **Storage** - This can be a big issue once you have been quilting for a while. All quilters accumulate large amounts of fabric; new fabric, left over fabric from previous quilts, fabrics waiting for a project, fabrics we fall in love with and can't resist. It all has to be kept clean and protected from creepy-crawly damage. I don't know any quilters who don't have fabric in large plastic boxes with lids stored under beds, in wardrobes, on bookshelves - any nook and cranny they can find. Think about how and where you might store your stash and start preparing. It WILL come.

Organising a dedicated quilting space

If you have outgrown or can't use the dining room table, you will need to create a space in your home dedicated to quilting. You must make decisions regarding what kind of work-centre you will have and what should go where to make the work flow easier and more comfortable.

Keep two things in mind - purpose and budget. You don't need a quilting palace, just a space where there is enough room to work, everything fits within easy reach, and you can find what you need, when you need it.

Before you start;

- Make a list of what you have already that can still be used,
- Make a list of what you need to acquire - not want, need. For example, if you have been cutting out on the breakfast bar, you may want to buy a cutting table,
- Prioritise your needs, a sewing table might be the most important purchase. You can continue to cut out on the breakfast bar for a while,

Don't expect to have the perfect quilting place straight away.

- Allow yourself time to try thing out.
- You'll know what's missing when you go to do something and you don't have the necessary tool.
- You'll know what kind of storage you need when fabric scraps or yardage overwhelm the sewing table.

As you gain confidence and master the skills of quilting, you will realise what tools you need to have within reach and which you can put away. As your working habits become more ordered and sophisticated, your work-space needs will change.

Happy Places evolve.

Over the sixty-plus years I've been sewing, where and how I sew has changed a lot. When I was a schoolgirl, I had a tiny bedroom. Therefore sewing was confined to the dining room table. I had to put everything away at the end of a sewing session, and to be very patient, especially with helpful grown-ups who liked to give unwanted advice! Bless 'em. I wish they were still here fussing about.

After I married, our first two homes were quite small and for many years, the dining room table and the breakfast bar were my work-spaces, and Saturday, when the kids played sport, was my sewing/quilting time. Later, when I had the luxury of a separate dining room, I could leave the machine set up. Luckily, my boys were happy to have meals on their lap in front of the TV any time.

Now, I'm not a neat freak. When I started sewing, my workspace was often in complete chaos and that hasn't changed. My storage gets messy and tangled, just like everyone else. However, it didn't take me long to realise that I needed to be more organised in my work area, or when it came to making space for cutting, or finding that ¼ inch foot, I was up the creek without a paddle.

That's when I discovered large storage boxes that fit under beds, folders that hold instruction sheets and fit on bookshelves, and Tupperware!

My next home was in Eumundi, an acreage property with more rooms than we needed (most of the time). I had space to create a dedicated quilting room. We planned and furnished it with a second-hand Horn cabinet found at an auction (it eventually fell apart), an old table, an office chair, an ironing board, a set of open cube shelves from Ikea, and an mobile clothes rack.

The sewing room doubled as an ironing room. It had everything: light, air, quiet and space... and a little bit of fame! We liked to travel overseas each year. Some good friends house-and-dog-sat for us. John was a sound engineer. Being computer based, he could work anywhere and often brought work with him.

We came home after six weeks in Europe to find that my happy place was an even happier place. Thanks to all the fabric, the timber walls and the carpet on the floor, the acoustics of the quilting room were perfect. A rather famous recording artist, of whom I'm a huge fan, came over and turned my quilting room into an emergency recording studio for a week. While the cat's away.... They could at least have waited until I came home!

In 2017, we left Eumundi and down sized to a retirement village. Now my happy place is the second bedroom in our Villa. When we have family or friends visit, their bed, a king single that converts to a queen, is needed. So, it had to stay, but the wardrobe houses my stash, plus my embroidery and art supplies.

This means that if you stay with us, you get a tiny amount of hanging space and one drawer! So travel light!

I already had a table, ironing board and chair, but little storage space. My first purchase was a set of cube storage shelves to replace the ones left at Eumundi, again from Ikea. They fit exactly inside the wardrobe and allow me to store my fabric rolled like bolts around the cardboard inserts from shirt packages, and stacked on their ends. I roll left over jelly roll strips around pieces of cut up pool noodles and lie them on the shelves - no creases, no folds and sorted by colour.

Bless Ikea and Aldi - they think of everything, including cost. My second purchase was an Aldi cutting table which I purchased for $199. It has a manual winder with which can lower to sitting height or raise to cutting height. It's now over 7 years old and going strong!

The next piece of furniture was a basic Horn sewing cabinet, with a gas lift. It isn't an all singing-all dancing cabinet with space for an overlocker and an attached cutting table.

It simply has a gas lift for my sewing machine, a front that opens and and a lid that lifts up and over to rest on it to form a sewing table.

Inside the front are containers for reels of thread, tools, a pin cushion, and other sewing necessities. The machine rises and I'm ready to go. Unless visitors are in residence, it stays open.

Recently, we installed peg boards in front of the cutting table. Wow! What a luxury! All my mats, rulers, rotary cutters, scissors and gadgets are right within reach whenever I need them.

My quilting room is not an interior designer's dream. It doesn't have the latest cabinetry, or a smart racks and storage shelving for everything quilting.

It was created on a budget, to suit the way I work and to make quilting easier for my physical abilities, which is what makes it my happy place!

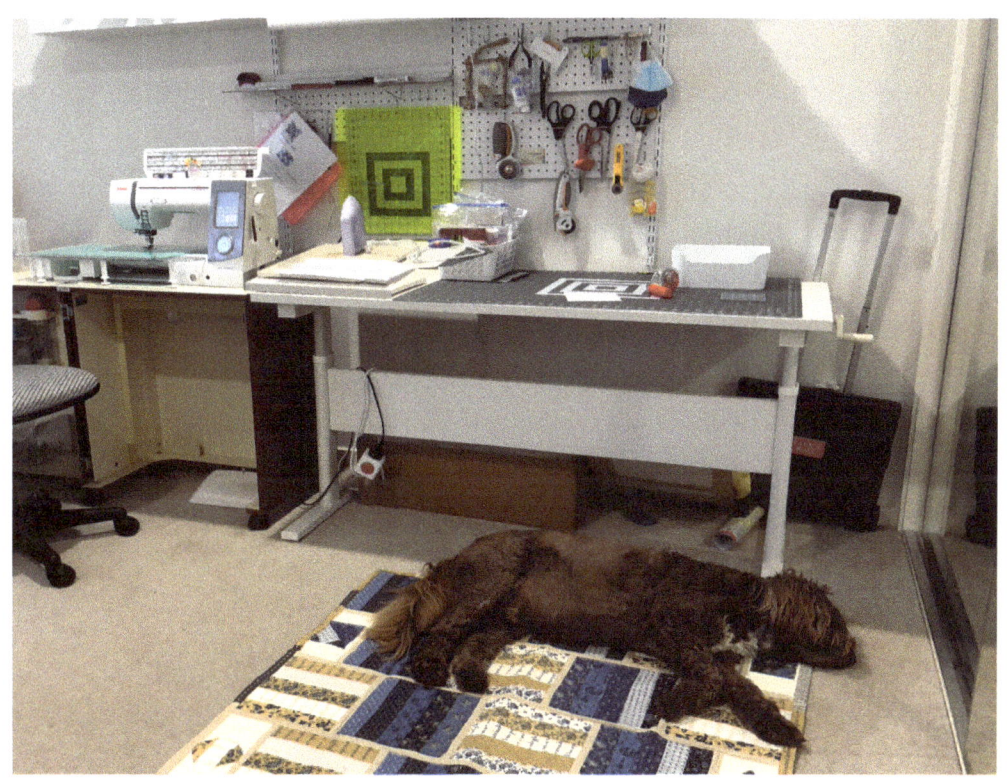

It's not fancy, but it's my Happy Place.
It's where my crazy labradoodle and I do what we most enjoy.
I cut and piece and quilt. He lies on his quilt and snoozes!

What if you can't create a space in your home to quilt?

For those of you who for various reasons can't set up your own quilting space, there are other options to explore.

- Quilting is a social activity as well as a sewing activity. Do not be afraid to call on other quilters in your community for advice.

- Find a quilting group. Many quilting groups meet in halls and community centres where they can take their machines and tools and quilt together.

- The University of the Third Age may have quilting classes or groups near you.

- Our local library has a sewing room that can be booked for periods of time. Talk to your local library and to community groups.

- If you live in a retirement village, check with your neighbours. There may be a craft or sewing room where sewing machines are set up for you to use and where other members of the community meet to quilt together. You may also find that quilting lessons are available.

Even if you have a great space at home, always remember that quilting is also a social activity. Quilters need to chat and share their experience, tips and hints.

It's good for the soul.

If you are unable to leave home to go to a quilters group, and you have a sewing machine or can hand quilt at home, there are ways to be with other quilters.

There are some groups of quilters who quilt in their homes , who prop up their mobile phone, iPad or tablet, turn on the video chat and work on their quilts, some on the breakfast bar, some on the table, others in a room at home, while being together as a group of friends. They stop for coffee and a social chat, and enjoy the benefits of a quilting social group right from home. What a great idea!!!

Wherever you are, whatever space you have, create your Happy Place.

Then you'll have every excuse in the world to say.

I CAN'T LEAVE MY
SEWING ROOM
BECAUSE I GET
DISTRACTED BY
ALL THE GOOD
STUFF I FIND

A quilt is a piece of art, the colours of the fabrics can make or break the beauty of the finished project. Many quilters find one of the hardest things to get their heads around is which colours go with what. Once you understand the way colours are formed, what creates a hue and a shade, or what colours compliment each other and which contrast, it is so much easier to mix and match your fabrics.

Okay, take a deep breath and let's dive in! It takes some concentration but believe me, it's worth it. Keep your eye on the colour wheel as we start on the outer ring with the hierarchy of colour.

1. **Primary**

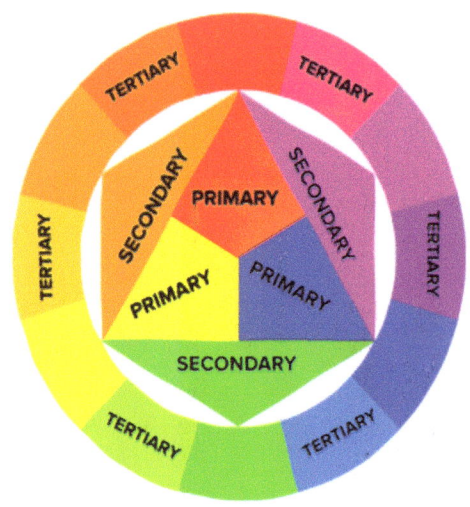

Primary colours are those you can't create by combining two or more other colours together. There are three primary colours: Red, Yellow and Blue. Think of primary colours as your parent colours. Knowing which primary colours create orange identifies colours that might go well with orange — given the right shade, tone, or tint.

2. **Secondary**

Secondary colours are the colours formed by combining any two of the three primary colours listed above. There are three secondary colours: orange, purple, and green, each created by using two of the three primary colours.

- Red + Yellow = Orange
- Blue + Red = Purple
- Yellow + Blue = Green

3. **Tertiary**

You create tertiary colours by mixing a primary colour with a secondary colour that comes next to it on the colour wheel. There are six tertiary colours t:

- Red + Purple = Red-Purple (magenta)
- Red + Orange = Red-Orange (vermillion)
- Blue + Purple = Blue-Purple (violet)
- Blue + Green = Blue-Green (teal)
- Yellow + Orange = Yellow-Orange (amber)
- Yellow + Green = Yellow-Green (chartreuse)

As you can see, not every primary colour matches with a secondary colour to create a tertiary colour. For example, red can't mix with green, and blue can't mix with orange — mixing these colours creates a muddy colour. But hey, if brown is what you are looking for - go for it!

Hues, tints, shades and tones.

Then there are brighter, lighter, softer, and darker colours you can create by mixing white, black, and grey with the original colours resulting in the following colour variations.

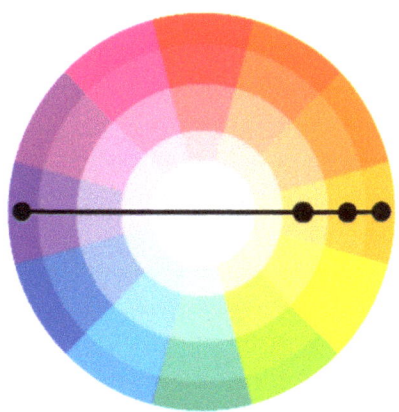

- Hue
  All the primary and secondary colours are "hues." Think of a hue as a child of a colour. If you combine two colours, for example blue and red, you have purple. If you want a hue of purple, a lighter purple, you need to combine hues of the primary colour - a light red and a light purple.
  This is because a hue has the fewest other colours inside it. By mixing two primary colours that carry other tints, tones, and shades inside them, you're adding more than two colours to the mixture — making your final colour dependent on the harmony of more than two colours. So mixing a tint of red with the hue of blue, and you'll get a slightly red-tinted purple in return.

- Shade
  You may recognise the term "shade" because it's used often to refer to light and dark versions of the same hue. However, a shade is the colour that you get when you add black to any hue. The various "shades" just refer to how much black you're adding.

- Tint
  A tint is the opposite of a shade, but people rarely distinguish between a colour's shade and a colour's tint. You get a different tint when you add white to a colour. So, a colour can have a range of both shades and tints.

- Tone
  You can also add both white and black to a colour to create a tone.

Using the Colour Wheel

The colours of a rainbow, in order, are red, orange, yellow, green, blue, indigo, and violet. Choosing colour combinations involves a much wider range than 12 basic colours. The colour wheel, which charts each primary, secondary, and tertiary colour, together with their respective hues, tints, tones, and shades, helps you choose colour schemes by showing you *how each colour relates to the colour that comes next to it on a rainbow colour scale.*

Colour experts and designers have identified seven common colour schemes. The seven major colour schemes are;

1. **Monochromatic**

"Monochromatic" is of one colour only. These colour schemes use *a single colour with varying shades and tints to produce a consistent look and feel*. Although it lacks colour contrast, it often ends up looking spotless and polished. It also allows you to change the darkness and lightness of your colours.

2. **Analogous**

Analogous colour schemes are formed by pairing one primary colour with the two colours next to it on the colour wheel. You can also add two additional colours (next to the two outside colours) if you want to use a five-colour scheme instead of just three colours. Analogous structures are *used to create a softer, less contrasting design*. For example, you could use an analogous structure to create a colour scheme with autumn or spring colours. This colour scheme is excellent for creating warmer (red, oranges, and yellows) or cooler (purples, blues, and greens) colour palettes.

3. **Complementary**

A complementary colour scheme is based on the use of two colours opposite each other on the colour wheel and relevant tints of those colours.

This colour scheme *provides the greatest amount of colour contrast*. Because of this, you should be careful about how you use the complementary colours in a quilt. It's best to use one predominant colour and use the second colour as an accent in your design.

4. Split Complementary

A split complementary scheme includes one dominant colour and the two colours next to the dominant colour's complement. This *creates a more nuanced colour palette than a complementary colour scheme*, while still keeping the benefits of contrasting colours.

5. Triadic

Triadic colour schemes offer high contrasting colour schemes while retaining the same tone. Create triadic colour schemes by choosing three colours that are equally placed in lines around the colour wheel.

Triad colour schemes are *useful for creating a strong contrast between each colour in a design,* but they can also be overpowering if you chose all of your colours on the same point in a line around the colour wheel.

Choose one dominant colour and use the others sparingly, or subdue the other two colours by choosing a softer tint.

6. Square

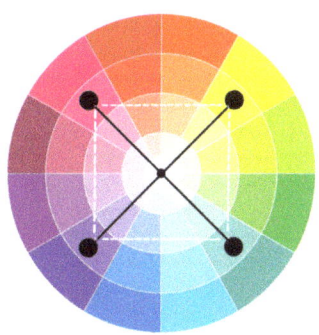

The square colour scheme uses four colours equidistant from each other (2 spaces apart and on the same circle) on the colour wheel to create a square or diamond shape.

While this evenly spaced colour scheme *provides substantial contrast to your design,* it's a good idea to select one dominant colour rather than trying to balance all four.

7. Rectangular

Also called the tetradic colour scheme, the rectangle approach is similar to its square counterpart but this time uses colour 3 spaces and 1 space apart. It *offers a more subtle approach to colour selection*. As you can see in the diagram, while the blue and red shades are quite bold, the green and orange on the other side of the rectangle are more muted, in turn helping the bolder shades stand out.

Applying the color wheel to fabric choice

Select a few different colour combinations using monochrome, complementary, and triad schemes to see what stands out. Get a sense of which scheme appeals to your personal perception and the look of your quilt. You may also find that schemes you select, which in theory look good, don't work with your quilt design. Trial and error helps you find the colours that both highlight and improve the look of the quilt.

Use the 60-30-10 rule.

Often used in home design, the 60-30-10 rule is also useful for quilt design. The idea here is to use three colours: A primary colour or tone for 60% of your design, a secondary colour for 30% of your design and an accent colour for the last 10%. While these aren't hard-and-fast numbers, they help give a sense of proportion and balance to your quilt by providing a primary colour with secondary and accent colours that all work together.

Create multiple colour sets

Create several colour sets for your quilt and see which one stands out. Take a step back, wait a few days and check again to see if your favourite has changed. Many quilters have a vision of what they want to see and what looks good. But what seemed like a perfect complement ends up looking drab or fussy. Don't be afraid to come up with a plan, throw that out and do another one, and another. Quilt design is a constantly evolving art. The more you play with colour, the better you get.

Consider the meaning of colours

Schemes are not the only consideration when choosing fabric colours. Along with varying visual impact, different colours also carry different emotional symbolism and create physical responses in human beings.

- Red is associated with power, passion, or energy, it's not for a restful quilt.
- Orange creates joy and enthusiasm, great for children.
- Yellow creates happiness and symbolises intellect.
- Purple gives a sense of luxury or creativity.
- Blue delivers tranquility and confidence depending on the shade.
- Lighter shades provide a sense of peace, darker colours a feeling of confidence.
- Green is often connected to growth or ambition.
- Black exudes an air of power and mystery.
- White symbolises safety and innocence.

Other Considerations

Who is it for? Is it a decorative quilt, bed quilt, baby quilt, bag, cushion? Have you fallen in love with a fabric pattern and want to use that as the base colour? Are you making a wedding quilt from the couple's favourite colour?

Which block are you using for the quilt? How many unique fabrics do you need for that pattern? Once you have chosen your main fabric, it's time to select other colours and patterns to bring out the best in it. The danger is in burying the main fabric in colours and patterns that shout over it.

What looks good? Look outdoors. Nature is the best example of colours that complement each other — from green leaves and the bright plumage of exotic birds to turquoise oceans and white clouds, you can't go wrong, taking colours from and combinations from the natural world.

What mood are you seeking? If passion and energy are your priorities, lean more toward red or brighter yellows. If you're looking to create a feeling of peace or tranquility, tend toward lighter blues and greens.

Think negatively. Negative space can help keep your design from feeling too cluttered with colour.

Colour context Contrast makes a difference to how we see colour. Look at these circles.

The middle of each circle is the same size, shape, and colour. The only thing different is the background colour. Yet, the colour of the middle circles appears softer or brighter, or may seem deeper, depending on the contrasting colour behind it.

65

Colour Tools

You've just examined a lot of theory and practical information to help you understand which colours go best together and why. But when it comes down to the actual task of choosing colours while you're shopping, it is always a great idea to have tools to help you do the work quickly and easily.

Luckily, there are tools to help you find and choose colours for your designs, particularly if you have access to a computer and a smart phone with a camera.

Adobe Color

One of my favourite colour tools to use while I'm designing quilts is Adobe Color. This free online tool allows you to build colour schemes from a fabric swatch. Once you've extracted the colours from a piece of fabric and used them to create a scheme you'd like, you can save it as a picture, add it to your phone photos and take it shopping with you. Adobe Color also features hundreds of pre-made colour schemes for you to explore and use in your own designs. Here's how it works.

1. Choose your feature fabric.

2. Take a photo of an area that contains all the colours on the fabric.

3. Open Adobe Color - http://color.adobe.com

4. Click *Extract Theme* and then *New*.

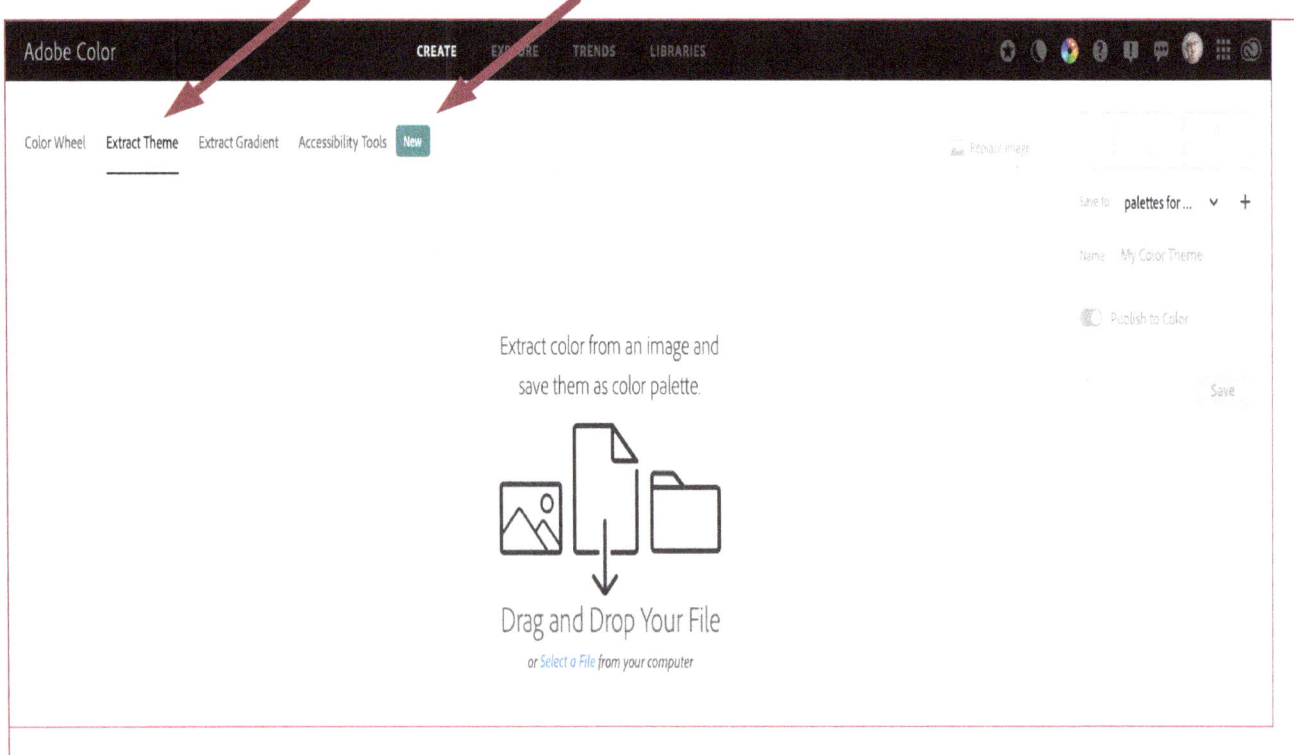

5. Drag the fabric photo into Adobe and click each of the different colour moods.

Save each colour palette and download it.

6. Click *Color Wheel*. Choose each type of scheme. Save each palette created as a photo.

7. Once you have all of the schemes on your computer, choose the one you like .

These are all the palettes that came from this fabric:

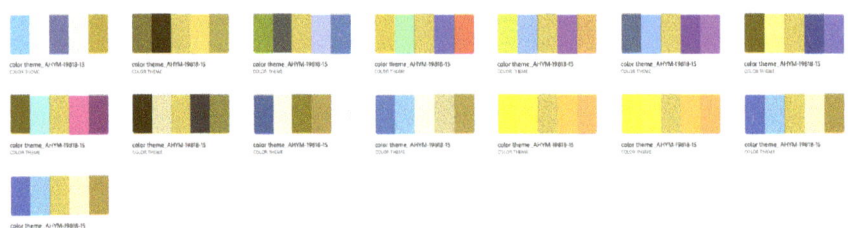

8. Have fun. Think about whether you want solid or patterned fabric. Look out for colours in the secondary fabrics that might disrupt the colour, or overpower the main fabric and discard them.

9. When you are satisfied you have a scheme that gives you the effect you want, go shopping, matching the fabrics to the colour scheme.

Of course, if you want the job done for you, consider some of the fabric collections that have been designed to go together. Moda, Robert Kaufman, Riley Blake and other manufacturers all have good quality, colour matched collections in their range. Your local quilt shop or the online quilt shops in your national marketplace will have co-ordinated designs from the major manufacturers in their range.

A word of caution, some collections are only available while stocks last.

If you decide to use a collection, make sure you buy all the fabric you need as soon as you have settled on a pattern and size for your quilt. There is nothing worse than getting 88% of your quilt completed only to find that you need 25cm more of one fabric and there is none left.

The quality of your quilt depends on the quality of your fabric. 100% crafting cotton holds its shape, and cuts and stitches easily. Good quality modern cottons are not prone to shrinkage and rarely colour-bleed. Cheaper cottons, particularly red may run. While you are learning, use less expensive fabrics. Fat flat packs of colour matched fabrics in shorter lengths are good value. However, if a quilt is to last a lifetime it must be good quality, colour fast cotton. You will pay more, but it's worth it.

Fabric choice - horses for courses

Quality fabrics cut more easily, hold their shape well, have less stretch and are easier to sew. There are specialist manufacturers who understand quilters' needs. When buying fabric for a special quilt look for such manufacturers as Moda, Kaffe Fasset, Robert Kaufmann or Riley Blake. They produce ranges of high quality fabric, in toning colours and patterns. Most good quilting suppliers stock these.

When you are making your choice:

- Feel the fabric. It should have substance and feel firm and durable.
  If it is thin, but stiff, it may have lots of size (a stiffener) in it and will wilt when washed.

- Tug the fabric on the diagonal (or bias) and see if it stretches easily.
  If it does, then it probably will move out of shape as you sew.

- Hold it up to the light.
  If you can see through it, the thread count is low and again it will pull out of shape, wrinkle as you stitch and feel flimsy in the quilt.

In quilting, you get what you pay for. Inexpensive is often going to give you a lower quality quilt. Very expensive is no guarantee of success either. You will learn, with experience, which fabric you can trust and which gives you a better finish and a cosier quilt.

Quilting improves your mathematics!

In Australia, we buy by the metre, half metre or quarter metre. However, the quilting world measures in yards, feet and inches.

To estimate how much fabric you will need, you need to convert from imperial to metric lengths before you go shopping. Specialist quilting shops have a significant advantage over stores like Spotlight and Lincraft.

Quilt shops are owned by and employ quilters .They can do all the conversion for you and advise you on which fabrics will do the best job. A beginning quilter's best friend is their Quilting Shop person.

Pre-cut Fabric

For those of us who have back problems, the fabric industry has produced pre-cut fabrics so we spend the minimum time bending over the cutting mat. There are many, many pre-cut fabrics.

Pre-cut fabrics were first mass produced by Moda who gave them names related to baking. Their Bake Shop website is full of great ideas for quilts using pre-cuts.

Each pre-cut is a pack of fabric pieces of the same size and shape. Most popular of the precuts are jelly rolls, layer cakes and charm squares.

Jelly rolls

A jelly roll is a bundle of pre-cut fabric strips that measure 2 ½" wide by 44"- 45" long.

Most jelly roll bundles contain 40 strips of fabric in a variety of coordinating colours and prints. There are junior jelly rolls containing 20 strips available. Dessert Rolls are a jelly roll with wider strips.

Layer cakes

A layer cake is a total of 42 pre-cut fabric squares. Each square is 10 inch by 10 inch. If there are 42 fabrics in the fabric design collection, you get one square of each fabric.

If the designer doesn't have 40 different fabrics in that particular collection, some will be repeated to have a total of 42 squares.

Charm squares

A charm pack is a bundle of 5" x 5" square of fabric. Depending on the fabric company, each Charm Pack normally contains at least one of each print in the collection. Most packs have around forty-two pieces, which means there can be duplicates and even triplicates of some prints.

All of these pre-Cut packs are also available in solid colours. I like to keep packs of junior jelly rolls, layer cakes and charm squares in white, cream. black, and basic shades of the primary colours. They make cutting 2" and 2 ½" squares quick and easy.

Fat flats and fat quarters

A fat flat or a fat quarter is a pre-cut piece of quilting fabric that is 22 inches (56cm) wide by 18 inches (46cm) high. It will usually then be folded in quarters. .A word of caution, fat flats and quarters are not the full width of the fabric.

If your instructions require you to cut strips that are the full width of the fabric, sometimes abbreviated to WOF (width of fabric), you will not be able to use fat flats or Flat Quarters, you should purchase whatever yardage you need off the bolt.

Fabric markers and erasers

A fabric marker is essential for creating guides on fabric and leaving no nasty marks! With a fabric marking pen and eraser duo, you will mark clear accurate lines onto your fabric, without bleed, and then use the eraser to make them disappear once you have finished. There are various kinds of water soluble eraser pens some are blue, some black, some pink. Air erasable and water soluble self erasing pens vanish after a period of time.

However, f you live in a humid climate, you will find that lines drawn with air erasable pens and self-erasing water soluble pens vanish very quickly, often before you have time to get to the sewing machine. The alternative, chalk pencils and chalk pounce pads work well. Bohin chalk pencils are my favourites.

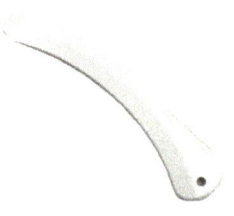

Another handy tool for marking fabric is the Clover Hera Fabric Marker Finger Presser. Using the sharp point at the top with a ruler makes an impression, providing a stitching guide without leaving a mark on the fabric.

Batting

Batting is the soft middle layer of your quilt, sandwiched between the quilt top and the backing. It is not something you can put inside a Doona cover, or the thick fluffy wadding you stuff into toys or parkas. It is a non woven fabric that gives your quilt warmth, comfort and dimension. Different types of batting can make a quilt flat or puffy, stiff or soft. It depends on what you want for your quilt. You can buy it by the metre, the roll or packaged pre-cut to a specific quilt size, e.g. cot, single bed, lap quilt etc.

Selecting Quilt Batting

Historically, batting was selected to provide insulation and warmth. If you pull apart a very old quilt you may find that old clothing or blankets, even sugar bags, may have been used as batting.

During times when a quilt's functionality meant everything, cotton or wool batting was used to provide insulation and warmth. Today, It is not a matter of choosing a favourite brand or style of batting for quilting. It may be tempting to select batting for your quilt based upon what happens to be on sale at the time. However, there is no all-purpose batting which works for every project. In fact, there is a great deal of variation in fibre, loft and construction. Batting should be selected to fit the needs of individual projects.

You need to think about the type of quilt, as well as your quilting method when you choose a batting. It helps to understand how manufacturers describe the features of their batting.

Batting terminology

- Loft
  Describes the height of quilt batting. The higher the loft, the thicker the quilt finish and the lower the loft, the thinner the quilt finish. Low-loft battings are a good choice for a flatter finish, where you want to show off the piecing more than the actual quilting lines.

- Scrim
  Most batting's have a scrim, a fine light weight non-woven fabric, the fibres of which are needle punched into batting. Scrim gives stability as the batting has less stretch. Scrim gives the batting strength and firmness, excellent for keeping your quilts in shape.

- Fusible batting
  This has a glue on the back and front. When heated with an iron it sticks to your quilt top and backing, basting your quilt layers. However, use a very good quality fusible batting as some less expensive ones leave a residue on your needle that transfers into the mechanical workings of the machine and builds up, creating damage.

- Insulated batting
  The heat-proof qualities make them ideal for placemats, oven gloves, pot holders, ironing board covers. If you use a piece of cotton batting either side of the insulated piece, you increase the protection even more.

- Bearding
  Fibres from the batting can pass through the quilt top and form a fuzz on the surface of the quilt. This most often occurs with cheaper polyester battings, but can also happen with cotton, wool and silk. Choosing a batting with scrim overcomes this problem.

Which fibre?

Batting is available in a number of natural and synthetic fibres. It is important to know the pros and cons of each.

- Wool batting
  Wool is easy to handle, and will certainly provide a great deal of warmth. However, it is more costly than cotton or polyester. Bearding is fairly common. Also, there is some risk of moth damage over time.

- Silk batting
  Silk is more expensive and difficult to find than cotton or polyester batting. Working with silk batting requires the use of special techniques. Machine quilting may be difficult, as silk batting may not cling well.

- Cotton batting
  Not all cotton batting is the same. Examine the batting for cotton seeds, as they can stain. If you are making baby quilts, or quilts for hospitals and care facilities, you MUST use cotton or wool batting. Polyesters do not breathe as natural fibres do and are harder to sanitise.

- Polyester batting: Polyester batts are less costly than many natural fibre ones. It's a good choice for anyone suffering from allergies. However, it does not breathe and is not suitable for babies.

- Poly-Cotton blend batting : Blended batting combines the best of both worlds. It is easy to work with, easy to care for and creates warm quilts.

Matching batting to your quilt

A major consideration in selecting batting is how the project is to be quilted. Some batting works well with either hand or machine quilting, while others work better for one technique.

- Natural fibre or blends, such as cotton and bamboo, work well for machine quilting. If you are quilting for a baby or for someone in nursing home, be sure to use cotton batting. Polyesters and other created fibres are often not acceptable as they do not 'breathe' and are harder to launder.

- The fabric used for a quilt backing can also effect your choice of quilt batting. Large prints or dark fabrics call for a more opaque batting. In particular, light-weight polyester batting is too sheer, allowing shadows from the backing to appear on your quilt top.

- A batting's construction method can also make it more useful for one type of project than another. Most cotton batting is stabilised by needle punching, which gives the batting a pad-like texture. While helpful for a sewing machine, this texture is difficult to hand quilt. Only the lowest loft cotton batting is manageable for quilting by hand.

- Yet another consideration is how well a batting clings to fabric. This is especially important for machine quilting, as it sets how close together the basting should be. For the most part, cotton batting clings well, whereas polyester batting does not.

- Finally, consider the use for which a quilt is constructed. Sturdy, washable batting is desirable for quilts that will receive frequent use, such as a baby quilt. Laundering and durability is less of a concern for decorative quilts.

Quality

Price is not always the best judge of quality. Even an expensive batting can let you down. A good quality batting of any loft, type or fibre should be stable and firm.

There are two Australian made products that are of high quality and available from shops and online. They are Hollybank and Matilda's Own. Both of these producers have all varieties of batting. They are more expensive than the imports available in some large stores and through e-Bay, and well worth the extra. They will not shrink, bead or push through to the outside of the quilt.

A good test for batting is to take it between your thumb and first finger on each hand and give it a gentle tug.

A good quality batting will have some give, but will not pull apart.

How much to buy?

Devoted quilters, those who have one or two quilts under the needle all the time, find that the most economical way to buy batting is by the bolt. When on special, a large bolt of good quality batting can be far less expensive than buying metreage or buying pre-packed lengths for one quilt at a time.

Batting sold by the metre is NOT the same width as fabric. Check the width of the batting you have chosen and calculate the amount you need to fill your quilt, plus an extra 25 cm to allow for the overhang if your quilt is for a bed.

If you are using the Quilt As You Go method, you will need the same amount of batting as you do backing.

The least expensive way to buy batting is definitely by the rill, BUT rolls of batting are heavy. It isn't kind to older quilters' backs and shoulders when it has to be pulled down from the shelf or when it's being rolled out for measuring and cutting, and it isn't kind to hands and shoulders when it has to be cut into 10" squares for QAYG blocks or 2" strips to support wide sashing. Even with the use of a long cutting ruler (those with a rolling blade attached to the side) it's a hard slog.

Nix panicus! Some bright manufacturers have come up with a solution. It's now possible to buy pre-cut batting in a wide variety of forms;

Quilt sizes - mainly in polyester, but there are cotton and wool-cotton blends available. You just have to find the right supplier. Search on Google there are a few online. The sizes available are;

- Cot 1 x 1.2
- Single Bed 1.5 x 2.2
- Queen size 2.7 x 2.4
- King-size 3.1 x 3.1
- Block size 10" squares - not available everywhere or all the time, but I have seen them on Etsy and eBay. Again, a Google search will find them. Just check the fibre and make sure you are getting good quality from a known manufacturer.
- 2" batting for sashing. Comes in rolls of 25 metres. Mainly advertised as jelly roll rug batting but great for giving stability to wider sashing.

Manufacturers are coming up with new products every day. Keep your eye on the quilting websites and such magazines as Quilting Daily and Fons & Porter.

Haberdashery

Thread

I prefer 100% cotton thread for quilting. However, there are some polyester threads, less expensive, and quite acceptable. There are some things you need to bear in mind.

- Some thread is better than others. Cheaper thread will break easier and could create a lint farm in your sewing machine. I don't buy the most expensive thread, but I don't buy the cheapest either.

- There is no need to buy thread that matches you fabric unless you are using it for topstitching your quilt. Neutral colours work well on most piecing projects – white, cream, beige or grey are all the colours you really need.

Pins

Quilters can never have too many pins! You will use them to pin your pieces together before sewing, so you will need plenty. You will also need different pins for different purposes.

Glass headed pins

Glass headed pins are a general purpose sewing pin - get these first.

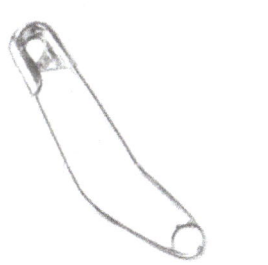

Curved safety pins

Curved safety pins are used to hold the layers of fabric firmly in place before and during the quilting process. They are easier to put through the sandwich and to open and close. An awl is really helpful when using bent safety pins.

Numbered pins

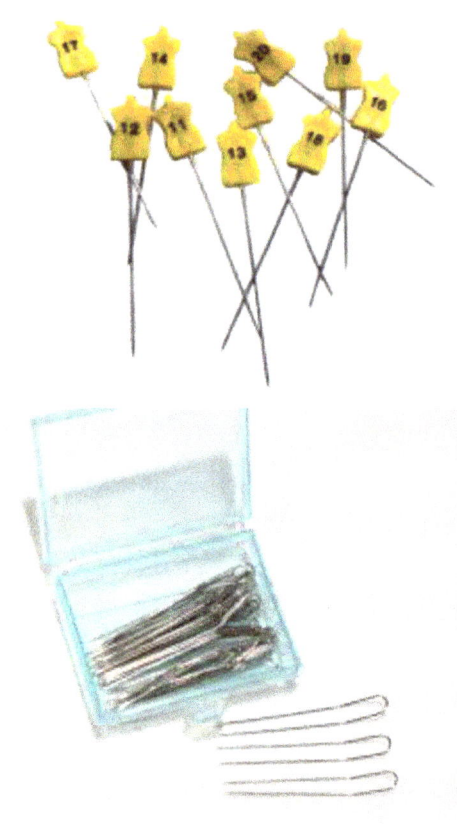

Numbered pins usually come in sets of five of each number. You use them to number each piece in a set of shapes, making it quicker and easier to follow the instructions

You can also number your blocks if you are following a sequence to make up a row in a quilt. Block 1 joins Block 2 then block 3. Numbered pins save a lot of unpicking!!!

Forked pins

My favourites are forked pins. They are very fine, sharp pins, double pronged like a hairpin.

They prevent seams moving during piecing and are handy for when you are making sashing and bias strips as you can use just the one pin to anchor both sides. The rounded end of the pin is raised, making them easy to insert and remove.

Forked pins are fabulous for holding pieces in place. They hold fabric firmly in place and you can sew over them without damaging the needle. You cannot beat them for sashing and binding.

And don't forget your pin cushion...

Pincushions like this one are filled with material to keep your pins sharp and dry, often sawdust. See how deeply the pins are pushed in. This keeps them safe from moisture. Rust is the enemy of sharps.

Others are made of foam rubber, careful of those, they can blunt your pins.

Our crafty ladies from the retirement village made pincushions on a square bathroom tile, which has fabric open bag hanging from it. They sit on the table beside teach sewing machine and we pop our waste thread into .it. Clever!

A pin cushion that fits on your wrist is fantastic. With one of these you won't have to worry about swallowing pins!

Sewing machine needles

Quilting needles have a slightly rounded point designed specifically for machine quilting and a slightly stronger shaft for stitching through multiple fabric layers. The point lets the needle go through the layers without leaving a permanent hole. It nudges the fibres aside rather than piercing through them. The deeper groove lets the thread slide freely through the many fibres of the batting.

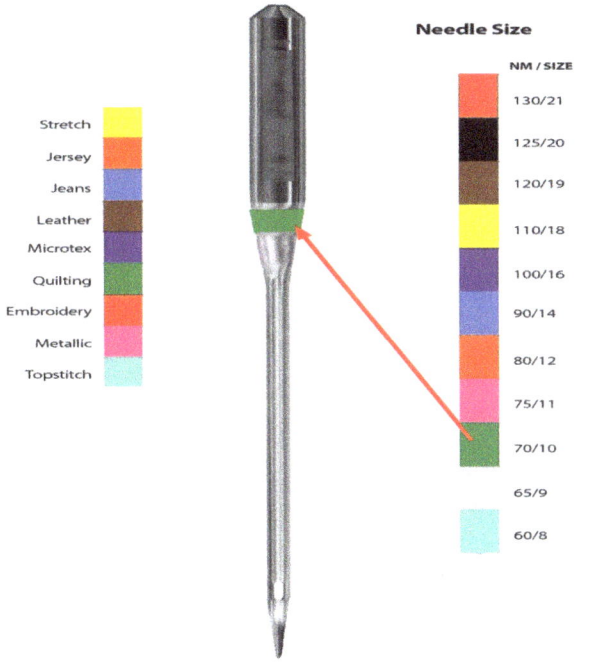

Consult your sewing machine's user manual and use the needles they recommend or choose a brand of needle that is recognised for quality and choose the ones recommended for your fabric.

One of the most common sizes of machine needles is 90/14. Its sturdy shaft holds up well when quilting through the layers of a quilt sandwich. The 90/14's needle eye is big enough to take most types of threads.

Use a 70/10 or 80/12 for intricate free motion designs and a 90/14 if your quilt sandwich is thick.

Schmetz colour code their needles to make your choice easier.

Caring for needles

Keep your needles in their packets or cases in a dry container, out of reach of little hands. If you are changing to a specialty needle for a specific task, store your regular needle in a pincushion, or their needle case, not in a drawer or on the floor.

Store your pincushion in a dry place when you aren't sewing - away from humidity. Have you ever wondered what the little strawberry on the side of one of those big strawberry pincushions is for? It's a needle sharpener! It's filled with iron filings.

Keep your needles and pins sharp by pushing them in and out of the little strawberry before you pop them in the pincushion. If you find you are having a problem with skipped stitches, take the needle between your thumb and first finger and run them down from top to bottom. If you feel any roughness or burr, change the needle.

You should always change your needle after 6 - 10 hours of sewing.

Put used needles and broken pins and needles in a sharps container.

You can up-cycle empty containers to safely store your used or broken needles and rotary cutting blades. Empty spice containers or pill boxes are strong, secure containers for used and broken pins and needles. Beverages like Cadbury's Drinking Chocolate come in a cardboard cylinder or tin with a plastic or metal lid and bottom. Cut a slot in the plastic lid and it makes a great container for used blades.

Machine bobbins

Some sewing machine brands, such as Brother, Juki and Janome recommend you use the bobbins made for their machines.

Check your sewing machine manual. If your machine is one of those brands, follow their advice. It will save you broken needles and tangled thread.

If your machine does not require the use of a branded bobbin, universal sewing machine bobbins will work for you.

Creating a quilt involves a number of steps.

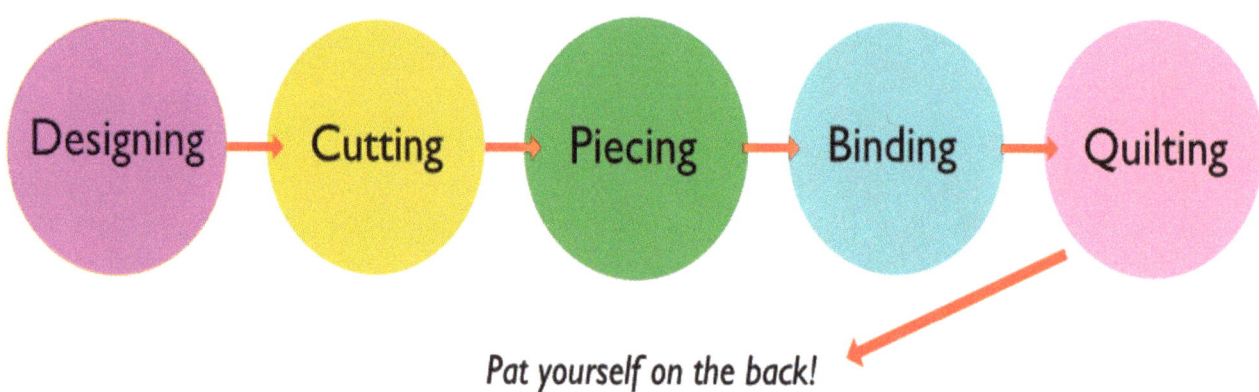

Pat yourself on the back!

Designing

You can design your quilt by combining the many traditional blocks that have been used in quilting over the centuries, as a free form art quilt, or you can follow one of the many patterns that are available from your quilt shop or online.

Traditional blocks

Some blocks are very simple, others are quite complex. All of them are based on basic geometry. Usually they are squares, but they can be circles, triangles or rectangles.

Whatever the shape, they are always a set number of inches and a half inch, for example 6 ½ " or 12 ½ ".

The extra half inch is to allow for a ¼ inch seam all round when sewing the blocks together to make your quilt.

Inside the blocks are various pieces of fabric, cut into shapes and sewn together, again with a ¼ inch seam, to form the block pattern.

For example, here is a traditional log cabin block. You can clearly see each piece of fabric that has been stitched around the square in the middle

To estimate how many blocks you will need, divide the area of the quilt by the size of the blocks.

For example

A cot size quilt is 23 inches x 46 inches.

A quilt of 6 inch blocks will need to be 4 blocks wide and 8 blocks long, which is 32 blocks altogether. If you use 10 inch blocks you will need 2 blocks wide and 4 blocks long, 8 blocks altogether Then you will add a 3" border at the top and bottom and a 6" inch border at the sides to cover the cot.

These are the standard sizes for Australian beds.

Bed	Length	Width
Single	87" - 106"	63"-81"
Double	87" - 106"	78"- 96"
Queen	92" - 112"	84" - 102"
King	92" - 112"	100" - 118"

When you work out your fabric yardage needs, remember to make provision for an extra half inch of length and width per block for the ¼ inch seam allowance. If you are in Australia, or New Zealand, you will need to convert the inches and yards to cm and metres. Don't panic. There are lots of tablet and phone apps that will work it out for you. And of course, your Local Quilt Shop has it all covered!

Free form art quilts

These are quilts that come from your imagination and sense of design. They can be very arty, or very simple. It all depends on your imagination, creativity and experience.

Here's how you might set out design your own pattern.

1. Have a picture in your mind of what you would like your quilt to look like.

2. Decide how big it should be, for example a cot quilt might be 36 inches x 60 inches finished, or a play mat might be 60 inches x 60 inches finished.

3. Decide on a block size. If your quilt is a 60" square, it could be made in 10" finished blocks, or 6" finished block. I'm lazy - I'd go for 10" blocks, so I would need 6 rows with 6 blocks in each row = 36 blocks altogether.

4. Decide what pattern block you want to use. Try to stick to straight lines if you are a beginner.
   Get some graph paper, preferably with a scale of 1 inch per square, or make your own by using baking paper and tracing over the lines on your cutting mat.
   For my play mat, each square would represent 10"

5. Try a few combinations and when you have what you like, take another piece of graph paper where each square represents an inch of your block

6. Draw your block. If you are like me, you may have to scrap a few drawings before getting it right. The eraser is as necessary in quilt design as the seam ripper is in sewing!

7. Calculate the size for each piece of your block, remembering to add ¼ inch seam allowance all round, and make a list of the pieces that you will need to cut.

I once found a pattern that I really loved in a magazine, I made up the first block, but it was all wonky. It took me try after try to finally work out the designer had forgotten to add the quarter inch all around to just one piece. Since then, I like to cut out the pieces of my block from the graph paper onto a smaller piece of baking paper, then use a ruler to draw a ¼ seam allowance around it, giving me the right size to cut.

8. Make a plan. How will the different sections of your block go together? Take note of the order of sewing to create your block. Label the pieces by shape, size and colour/pattern.

9. Write out your pattern, numbering each step. You may want to draw pictures or diagrams to help you remember the process.

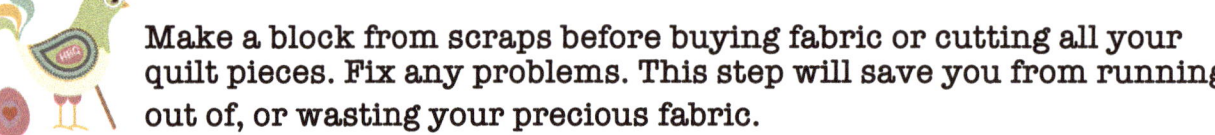

Make a block from scraps before buying fabric or cutting all your quilt pieces. Fix any problems. This step will save you from running out of, or wasting your precious fabric.

Calculate how much fabric you will need.

Go back to your plan, work out how many blocks you will get out of the width of the fabric (WOF). My play mat calculations for backing and sashing are;

Metric (For the Aussies and Kiwis)

- Width of fabric = 110 cm
- 110cm divided by 26.7 cm = approx. 4 blocks to WOF with a smidge left over.
- 9 rows of 27.7cm of fabric = 248.4 cm or 2.48 metres

I would buy 2.5 metres for the backing if I was making a QAYG quilt plus an extra metre for sashing = 3.5

Imperial

- width of block = 10 ½" (includes seam allowance) = 26.7 cm
- 40 inches divided by 10 ½ inches = 3 blocks with 3 4/5 inches left over.
- 36 blocks needs 12 rows of 10 ½ inches of fabric = 126 inches = 3.5 yards

I would buy 3.25 metres for the backing if I was making a QAYG quilt plus an extra ½ yard for sashing - I'd use the left over width for row sashing.

Working out the fabric for the component pieces of the block is much the same. There is another advantage to making the block from Fat quarters of inexpensive fabric. You can see from the result how much of the quarter is used for each piece, which will give you a rough idea of how much you will need for however many blocks you needs to make.

For example if you have to cut a 5 ½ inch square in a particular colour, you can get four 5 ½" squares out of 40" WOF (7 out of 110cm)

If you need 36 of the squares, to work our how many rows you need to cut divide 36 by 4, which equals 9 rows of four squares. 9 x 5 ½ = 49 ½ inches = just over 1 1/3 yards. You would buy 1 ½ yards.

If you live in Australia you need to calculate in metrics, you would get 7 blocks to a row, divide 36 by 7, you would need 6 rows = 160.2cm, just over a metre and a half. You would buy 1.75 metres for the squares.

If you feel this is all too much to do - you can find a quilt pattern from a book, a magazine or online and it will tell you how much fabric you need, what pieces to cut and how to assemble it.

PLEASE make a test block first, even professional quilt designers can get it wrong - and remember if you're in Australia and the fabric quantities are in US measurements, you will need to convert from yardage to cms and metres.

... Let's get cutting!

Accurate rotary cutting is essential for successful quilts and quilt blocks. The key is practice, practice, practice. A practice block, rotary cut, sewn and assembled BEFORE you start to cut out the blocks for a queen bed quilt in expensive quilting fabrics will save you a lot of heartache not to mention heaps of money.

Cutting

Measuring and cutting are the most important parts of making a a quilt. If your measurements are incorrect, or your cutting is not straight and true, your quilt will not come together as you planned. Here are some hard and fast rules that will ensure your cutting is as safe, accurate and correct as you can make it.

The Golden Rules of Cutting

1. **Use a cutter that is comfortable and suits your hand, arm and shoulders.**
2. **Use a cutter with a sharp blade.**
3. **Practice cutter safety.**
4. **Always use an acrylic quilting ruler.**
5. **Never use a rotary cutter on any surface other than a self healing cutting mat.**
6. **Turn the mat, not the fabric.**
7. **Always cut away from yourself.**
8. **Attach gripping tabs to the bottom of rotary rulers.**
9. **Press before cutting.**
10. **The more fabric you stack, the less accurate your cutting.**

Let's unpack each of the rules. What do they mean?

Rule 1 - Choose the right cutter for you.

There are rotary cutters and rotary cutters. It's the most important tool in your box, along with your ruler so don't buy the cheapest one you can find. When you cut, you use you whole hand, wrist and arm - constantly. The more pressure you have to put on the cutter to get through the fabric, the more wear and tear on you.

Choose a cutter that is comfortable to hold, that cuts smoothly and cleanly, that has a good safety shield over the blade and, if you are left-handed, converts to left handed, or has a left handed version.

If you have hand, wrist, arm or shoulder pain, choose an ergonomic cutter that allows you to keep your wrist straight and loose and requires only moderate pressure to cut through two layers or more of fabric. There are a number of good quality ergonomic cutters available, Fiskars has two stick cutters that are convertible to left hand users. Martelli makes left and right handed versions of their ergonomic cutters, but the one I find most suitable for older quilters with hand and wrist challenges is the TrueCut Comfort Cutter. Combined with their rulers it's a perfect system for us oldies.

Rule 2 - Keep your blade sharp

Every rotary cutter blade will eventually begin to wear. It's like a car tyre, the more you drive it across the road surface, the more the rubber wears away. The more you drive your blade through the fabric and across the cutting board surface, the more the fine edge wears down. You can tell when your blade needs sharpening or changing. It creates a tendency for the cutter to swerve, which can be dangerous. Bandaids on the fingers are a good sign of a blunt blade.

Once you have completed the equivalent of a full size quilt, you will probably need to change or sharpen the blade on your rotary cutter. Some blades cannot be sharpened, but if they can, it will save a lot of money in buying new ones. Rotary blades require a sharpener specifically designed for the job.

These vary from manual sharpeners to electric sharpeners. If the blade has to be removed from the cutter to be sharpened, check the shape of the hole in the middle of your blade and make sure that the sharpener takes that blade. If you have hand, wrist or arm issues, an electric sharpener, similar to the TrueCut sharpener will suit you best. It takes most blades and is easy to use.

Rule 3 - Cut safely

Rotary cutters are VERY sharp

- Always close the cutter and keep the blade covered with the safety shield when you are not cutting. I've known quilters who forgot this rule, like one who leaned over their cutting mat to reach the pincushion, put a hand out to steady herself without looking and needed nine stitches in her palm.

- When holding your ruler steady keep your fingers at least an inch away from the cutting edge. If the cutter hits a pin hiding under the fabric and jumps, it's easy to lose a chunk of finger.

- When changing a blade, use tweezers to remove the old blade and replace it with a new one.

- Use a 60" cutter if you want to cut through more than two thicknesses of fabric.

- Put the cutter down, closed, before you attend to anything else.

- Don't scratch your nose with an open cutter in your hand.

Rule 4 - Use a ruler made for the job

Acrylic rulers have all the markings and measurements for quilting and have a strong, straight edge to guide you.

If you have a slight tremor, or find it hard to cut straight along the ruler without veering off, there is a ruler that could have been made just for you. TrueCut rulers have a built in track on the edges and a guide on the comfort cutter that ensure a straight cut to suit even the wobbliest hand. Wooden rulers are dangerous. Rotary cutter blades are extremely sharp and can slice through the wood and into your hand. Metal rulers are not transparent and are so narrow that the blade may slide across and cut you.

Rule 5 - Use a cutting mat

The dining room table or the breakfast bar might be great places to cut, but they are NOT the right surface to cut ON. You will either ruin the dining room table or destroy your rotary cutter blade on the stone surface. Self healing cutting mats are made for the job. Most cutting mats have measurements printed on them, however, it is wise to rely on your ruler rather than the mat for measuring the lengths and widths of your pieces before you cut. Your ruler is precise, the mat may not be.

First and foremost, the mat is for protection of the cutting table and the cutter.

Rule 6 - It's easier to cut straight and true if you turn the mat not the fabric.

When you need to to make a second cut in the same piece of fabric, for example to cut a square into four triangle, turning it will move the fabric out of line and cause a change in the size or shape of each piece.

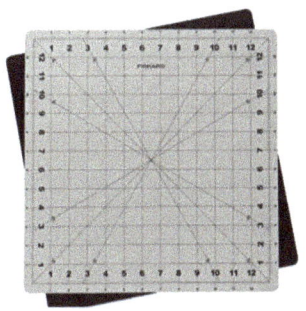

Carefully turning the mat keeps the fabric in place ensuring that your cut is straight and true. For this type of cutting, use a smaller mat that can be easily rotated. There rotating mats (they sit on a turn table) available that to enable you make multiple cuts without needing to lift the fabric.

Rule 7 - Cut in the right direction and at the right height

The correct direction to cut fabric is straight ahead, from the bent elbow at your waist push the cutter forward away from you in a straight line along the edge of the ruler.

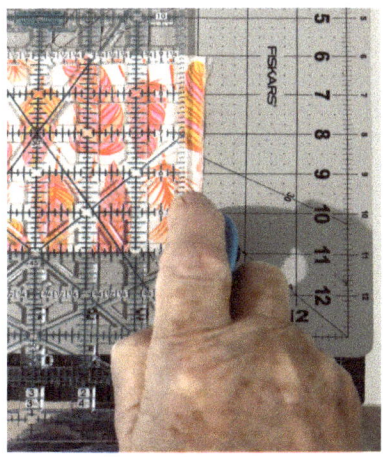

If you are right handed, this is the right hand side of the ruler, if you are left handed, the left side of the rule.

There are times when you are tempted to cut when your fabric or cutting board is at angle to you. Don't be tempted. Cutting across your body or away from your body may cause the cut to be offline, veer away from the ruler or over the ruler towards you hand. In any event, it doesn't make for accuracy.

The other important factor is the height of your cutting table. If you are tall, cutting at table height, means that your cutting surface is too low and you are constantly bending over to cut. The breakfast bar, or office desk height will be closer to the right height for you. If you are short, table height, breakfast height or desk height may be too high. If so, try to find one of those low steps that gym users have for stepping exercise. Standing on one of those may give you a better cutting height.

 The most useful table that you can have in your sewing room is a sit/stand table. It has a handle on the side that winds the table top up or down to suit your needs. I use mine to sit when I cut. I have hip and back challenges and can't always stand to cut. By moving it up and down as necessary I avoid a lot of pain and can cut accurately from the waist all the time.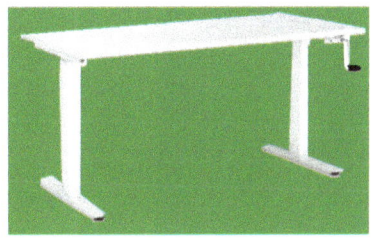

If you suffer from arthritis, spondylitis, hip and back joint pain, you can find these at a reasonable price from Ikea. I found mine at Aldi.

Rule 8 - Use gripper tabs or tape on the bottom of your rulers

Because they are acrylic and smooth rulers will slide around on the fabric. No matter how firmly you press down your ruler will move slightly off the line, giving you a less accurate cut. The best way to prevent this happening is to put gripping tape or tabs on the bottom of the ruler. It's your choice as to which ones you use, but I find that tape gets in the way unless it is super clear. Tabs (spots) are better.

Place them evenly across the back. If you can, choose areas where there is no number or measurement mark. If they start to yellow or ooze sticky, take them off, clean the area and replace them.

I have tried a number of brands, but once again, TrueCut seem to have come up with the best in TrueGrips: crystal clear and so far, I haven't had any move, fall off, go yellow or ooze.

Rule 9 - Press your fabric before cutting

Any crease or wrinkle in your fabric is going to create a problem. It is so easy to thin you have cut a straight line when in fact there was a tiny fold on the edge of the fabric that you couldn't see and when you stitch the seam, the shape is out a puffteenth of an inch and the whole block is wonky.

Smooth, crisp fabric cuts better, If you are using a very soft fabric, it helps to spray it with a little starch or stiffener before you attempt to cut.

Rule 10 - Be patient, don't try to cut too much at once.

Some quilt patterns tell you to stack strips before rotary cutting them into smaller shapes, or it's fine to cute four to six layers of fabric at a time. It is. It's okay. I do it all the time.

However, I use a very sharp 60mm rotary cutter. If you are going to cut more than 2 layers you need to have a cutting surface wide enough to handle them.

If you do have a 60mm cutter and you want to stack layers of fabric, line them up very carefully and hold the ruler down firmly so that it does not move. The spaces in the TrueCut rulers are great for this, as you can place some of your fingers through the holes onto the fabric and others on thee ruler. Both fabric and ruler are held firmly.

There is another aspect to this rule. Standing all day in an effort to cut a whole quilt's worth of fabric is silly. Our ageing bodies aren't meant to stand all day. Sure as the sun rises in the morning, your back, arms and shoulders will give you curry the next day and you won't be able to sew. Pace yourself. Cut a few blocks at a time and assemble them. Cut a little, sew a little. Stop for a chat and a coffee. Quilting is meant to be social and fun.

Putting the rules to work.

Square up your fabric before cutting

It's important to square up one end of the fabric before you rotary cut the long strips required for a quilt pattern. After squaring up, the leading edge should be a 90-degree angle to the fold. *If you are left handed, work from the opposite side of the fabric, placing fabric and rulers in mirror-image positions.*

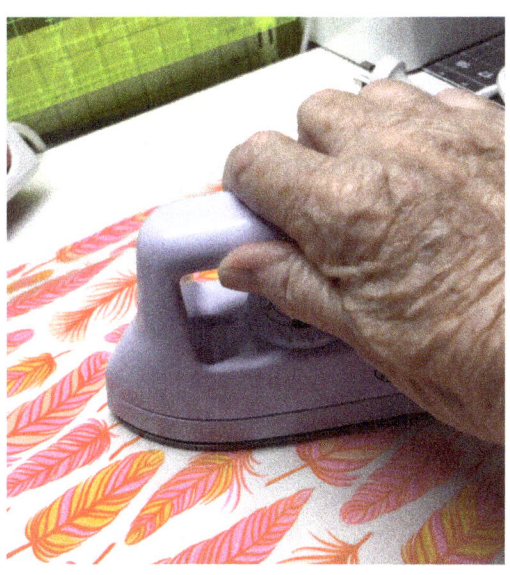

1. Lightly press the fabric to get rid of any creases. Fold the fabric along its length, selvedges together. The fold should be straight, with no puckers. selvedges might not be perfectly aligned at the end of the fabric, but that's okay; it's most important for the fold to be accurate.

2. If you are working on a small rotary cutting mat, you may need to fold the fabric again, making it four layers deep. Beginning quilters should stick to one fold because each new fold makes inaccurate cuts more likely.

3. Place the fabric on a rotary mat with the fold near the bottom edge of the mat and the side to be squared on the left.

4. Place the ruler on the fabric. A horizontal line on the ruler must be exactly matched to or parallel to the fold.

5. Place your hand on the ruler to hold it firmly in place. Spread your fingers out to hold the ruler securely, but take care to keep fingers out of the path of the cutter.

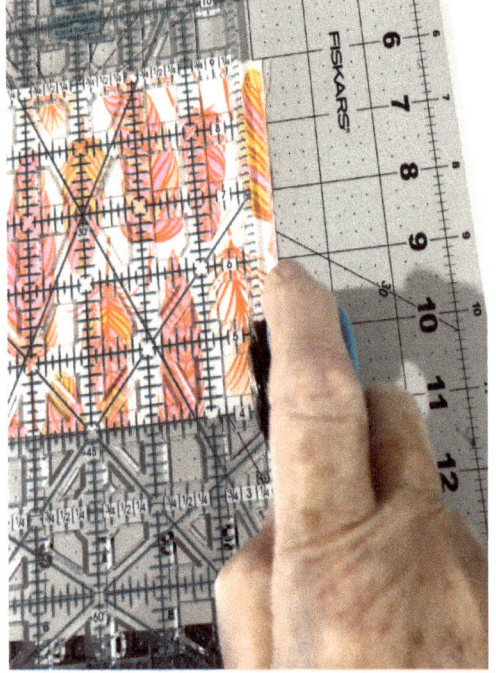

6. Roll your rotary cutter from bottom to top along the ruler's right edge. The fabric's cut edge should now be at a 90-degree angle to the folded edge. Once your fabric is squared up, you are ready to cut your pieces.

It isn't unusual for the leading edge of the fabric to move out of square after several cuts. Before you make each cut, check the left and bottom edges of the fabric align with vertical and horizontal markings on the ruler. If not, square up the end again before cutting more strips.

Cutting fabric on the bias
In this exercise we are using purchased bias binding, but you can make your own.

1. Long bias strips are sometimes used to make quilt binding and for appliqué shapes that bend easily into graceful curves, such as flower stems.

2. To cut bias strips of fabric, align the 45-degree mark on a long rotary ruler with the fold in the bottom of the fabric. Hold the ruler in place and cut along its right edge.

3. To make the next cut, align the correct line on your ruler with the angled edge of the fabric and the 45-degree line with the fold. Rotary cut along the right side of the ruler again. Continue until you have the number of strips required.

Piecing the quilt

Time to sew! But before we do, here's a reminder of some terms that you will come across.

- Selvedge means the tough ½ inch ends of the fabric (sometimes printed with information about the fabric).
- Raw or cut edge means the edge of the fabric where the fabric has been cut or torn.
- Bias means at an angle. When you cut across fabric at any angle except exactly 90 or 180 degrees to the selvedge, you create a bias edge. Bias edges are despised in quilting because they are stretchy and lose their shape when handled or sewn.
- If you cut your fabric perfectly on the straight of grain - 90 or 180 degrees to the selvedge - your edges will hold their shape better. For perfect 5 inch squares, carefully avoid creating any bias edges by cutting on the straight of grain.
- WOF (width of fabric) is the distance from selvedge to selvedge, which is usually about 44 inches for quilting fabric.
- Scant ¼ in You will sometimes hear quilters talk about a "scant ¼-inch seam". A scant ¼-inch seam means something just less than ¼ inch. It takes into account the tiny fold of fabric you lose when you sew a seam and then fold it over and press it. If you are following a pattern and finding that your blocks are turning out just puffteenth smaller than they are supposed to, try sewing a scant ¼-inch seam instead of a true ¼-inch seam.

A word about seams

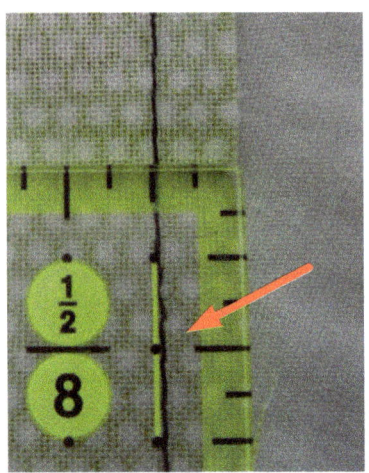

In quilting we sew with a ¼ inch seam. Sounds simple, but it can be a little tricky.

The generic foot that comes with most sewing machines usually sews a ¼ inch seam if you line up the fabric at the edge of it. However, some sew a 3/8 " seam. You will not know what your machine sews until you try it. If it sews the wider seam, depending on your machine, you may want to purchase a ¼ inch foot.

Blocks that are not true to the size that you intended to have in your design are the consequences of sewing the wrong size seam.

Here's an example.

You'll notice that the squares don't line up. The top row of squares was stitched with 1/8 inch seam, it was 1/8 inch too wide, leaving each square ¼-inch too small.

The bottom two rows had the ¼-inch seam stitched and line up perfectly. If this had happened all the way through the quilt everything would have been completely out of kilter.

Let's make a small quilt

If you are an experienced quilter, especially if you already use Quilt As You Go techniques, you can skip this exercise if you wish. However, if you don't, you might pick up a hint or two that adds to your quilting tricks box. (Look out for the Old Chook.)

The first step in making a quilt is to plan. For this exercise the plan is;

1. What are we making? A mug mat.

2. Do we have a pattern? Yes.

3. What fabrics do we need?

   - A fat quarter each of five different but matching patterned fabrics (or 5 charm squares and a fat quarter of toning fabric).
   - A piece of batting - thermal batting wold be good but any batting will do.
   - Bias binding.

The next step is to gather the tools you need;
- Cutting mat
- Rotary cutter
- Ruler
- Iron and ironing board
- Sewing machine
  - Machine correctly threaded with neutral thread
  - Bobbin loaded with the same neutral thread

Now, close the book and go and find/buy your five fat quarters of different but coordinating patterns or shades and some batting and half a metre of matching bias binding.

When you have them,
- set up an ironing board and iron
- place your cutting mat on the table/bench top,
- grab your ruler and rotary cutter, and it's...

Ready...

Following the cutting rules and steps,

- Cut five 5 inch squares, each a different pattern in toning colours. (Skip this if you are using Charm Squares)
- Cut one 9 ¼ inch x 8 ¼ inch rectangle of one of the toning fabrics
- Cut one 9 ¼ inch x 8 ¼ rectangle of batting - set to one side

Set...

The front will consist of two 5 inch squares of fabric and five 2.5 x 5 inch rectangles. Gather your 5 coordinating squares and decide how you would like to have them arranged on the front of your mug mat. The back will consist of the 9 ½ inch square.

- Take three of the squares and cut them in half to make six 5 inch x 2 ½ inch rectangles.

There is a short cut to cutting 3 squares in half at once.

- Place the squares one on top of the other, making sure that the sides and corners match.
- Measure 2 ½ inches from the left side of the squares.
- Using a 60mm rotary cutter, cut firmly along the ruler. You now have six 2½x5 inch rectangles. You only need 5. Choose one each of 5 pattern and put it and the rest of the strips to one side.

Sew ...

The front

Place the two left hand strips face to face and pin them together on the right hand long side .

- Place the two right hand strips face to face and pin them together on the right hand long side.

- Take both pinned pieces to the sewing machine. (Make sure you have your ¼ inch foot attached)

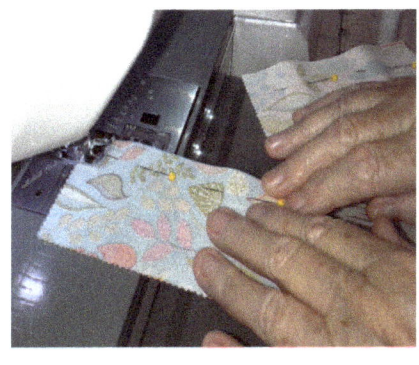

- Sew the left hand pieces of fabric, right sides together, along the pinned side using a ¼ inch seam allowance.

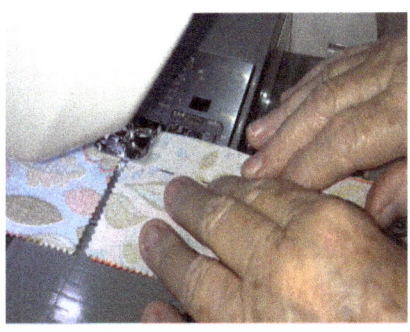

- When you reach the bottom, stitch 2-3 extra stitches then place the other pinned strips under the front of the foot and continue to stitch, down the pinned side with a ¼ inch seam.

- Remove the joined pieces and snip the joining thread.

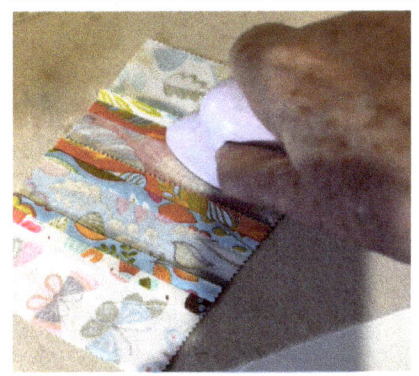

- With the wrong side up, press each seam open.

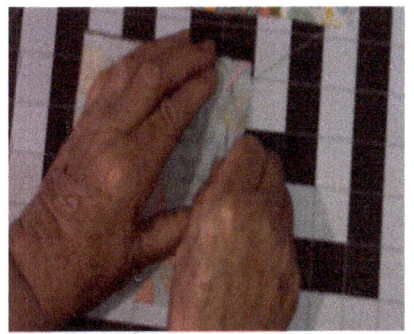

- Take the remaining two 5 x 5 squares, pin them right sides together on one side.

- Take them to the sewing machine and sew them together using a ¼ inch seam allowance.

- Press the seam open.

- Next take the fabric strips rectangle you just finished and the 2 squares you joined.
(The squares block will overhand the strips block at both ends.

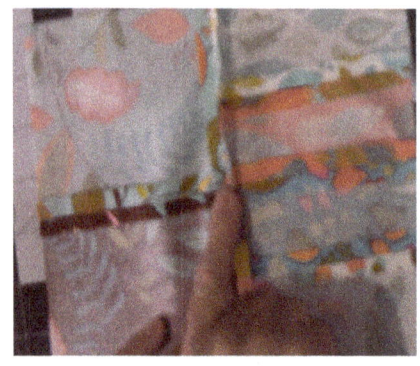

- Pin the bottom of the strip block to the top of the squares block on the long side with right sides facing

Make sure you match the centre seam on both blocks.

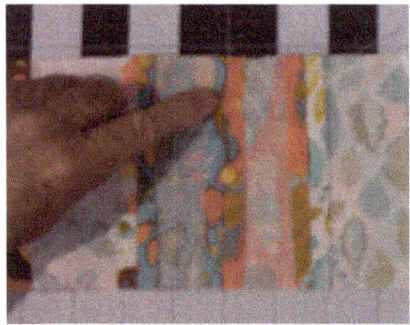

- Sew them together along the pinned side.
- Finger press the seam open.
- Press the seam back and front

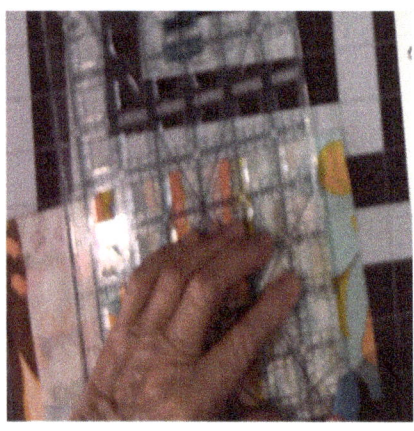

- Trim the new block;
- Line your ruler up with edge along the right side of the top half (strips) of the bloc.
- Trim the overhang off the bottom half (squares).
- Turn the block 180 degrees (The strip half is now at the bottom.)
- Line up your ruler along the edge of the bottom half.
- Trim off the overhang from the top half. (Squares)

You have now finished the front piece!

Now grab it, the batting and the back piece and …

Assemble the mug rug

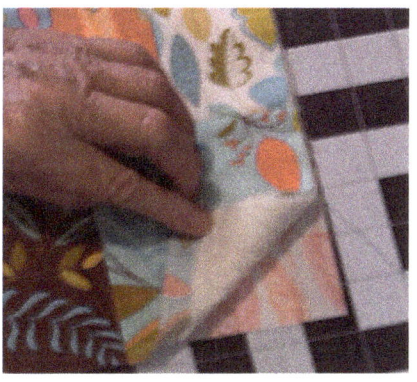

- Take the piece of cotton batting and sandwich it between the front and back pieces, making sure both pieces have their right sides facing out.

- Pin to keep the batting from moving while sewing the next step.

Quilt

For this next step you may want to use your ruler and marking pen and draw guide lines every half inch across the mug. However, there may be an accessory for your machine to save you this step.

The quilting bar

Look amongst your accessories for a round bar, about 60mm long with a hooked end, It slides into a hole towards the back of the presser foot holder. The hook should face towards you.

On the plate you should see some measurement lines, 3/8 inch ¼ inch, ½ inch, Each line indicates the space between the needle and the line. If you slide the quilting bar in until the hook lies along the ½ inch bar, there is a ½ inch space between the needle and the hook.

You can then sew a line ½ inch away from a seam, the edge of the fabric or a line you have already stitched.

If you have a quilting bar, put it on your machine and use it to measure the ½ inch quilting lines in the following quilting instructions.

Take your mug mat sandwich to the sewing machine.

Let's quilt

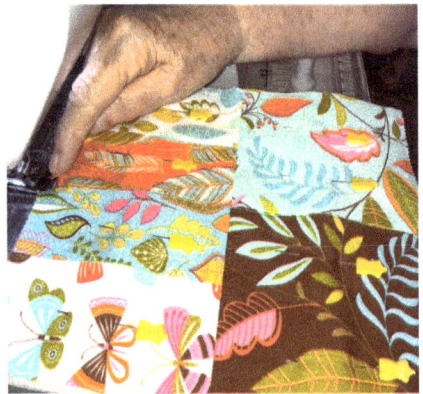

- Place the mug mat, front side up, under the raised presser foot with the strips at the top and the squares at the bottom.
- Slide it sideways until the needle is exactly over the centre seam of both the strips and the squares.

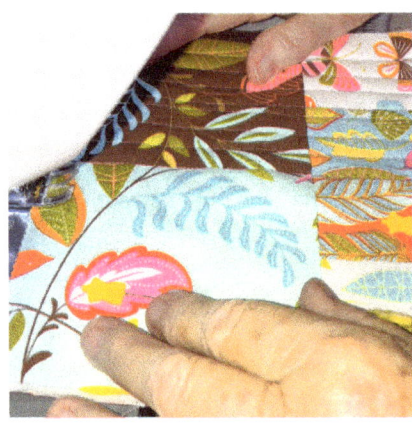

- Lower the presser foot
- Sew a straight line down the centre seam from top to bottom. Cut the threads.

- Lift the presser foot and slide the mug mat up to the needle.
- Move the rug ½ inch to the right from your centre line, place the hook of your quilting bar on the line you have just sewn.
- Lower the presser foot and sew another straight line.
- Continue sewing straight lines every ½ inch until you have quilted the first half of the mug rug.
- Turn the mug rug around 180 degrees

Place your needle ½ inch to left of the centre line and repeat the straight line process until the second half is quilted.

The next step is to bind it.

Binding - First square up your mug mat.

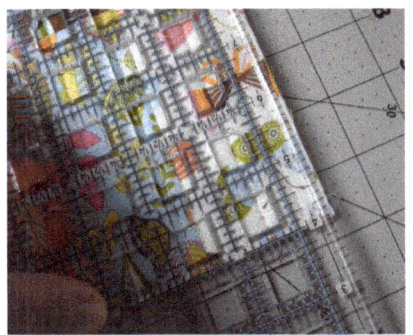

- This is best done with a 10 ½ inch or larger square ruler. Your mug mat is not a square, but using a square ruler allows you to check that each corner is a right angle corner - 90 degrees
  - Place the top right hand corner of the ruler on the top RIGHT hand corner of your mug rug.
  - Adjust the ruler so that a vertical line lines up with one of the seams on the strips.
  - If the corner is square the edges will line up with the edge of the ruler and the vertical line.

If the edge of the mug mat is not straight;

- Keeping a vertical ruler line running straight down the seam, using the rotary cutter, trim the right side of the square.
- Turn the cutting mat 90° to the right, keeping the ruler in place on the rug. The corner of the ruler should now be at the bottom right corner of the rug.
- Clean up the right edge of the mug rug by cutting off any excess.. Turn the cutting mat 90° to the right again.
- You now have two straight edges that are at the bottom and left side of the mug rug.
- Again place the ruler with the top corner of the ruler at the right hand side of the mug rug. The numbers should run from right to left starting at 1 on the right.
- Slide the ruler across the mug-rug until the horizontal line indicating 9 ¼ inches is lined up along the left edge of the mug rug. Using your rotary cutter trim the right side. Turn the mat 90° to the right.
- Using your square ruler, slide the ruler until the horizontal line indicating 8 ¼ inches is against the left edge of the mug mat and trim.
- All your sides should now be straight and your corners square.

Your mat is now ready for binding.

Bias bindings are made of different materials and may be folded in half, or only folded at the edges.

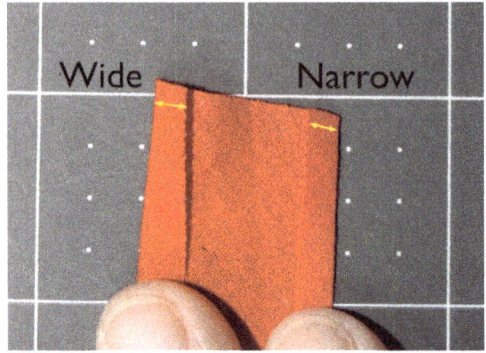

- Take your bias binding and open it up. There is a fold on each side of it.

Look at the folded bias binding from the back. One side is ever so slightly narrower than the other.

- If your bias binding is like mine, only folded at the edge, fold it in half, right side out and press it. Be careful, do not have you iron too hot or this will be the result.

 **Forked pins make binding much easier. Use Roxanne Glue first, then pin. You can sew right over them. Binding becomes easy-peasy.**

- With front side up, and the wider side of the binding to the front, Line up the centre fold of the binding with the raw edge of the mat. Fold the binding over the sides.

- Roxanne Glue, dotted along the edge of the mat makes binding much easier. A side at a time, dot the glue along the edge on both sides, then press and pin.

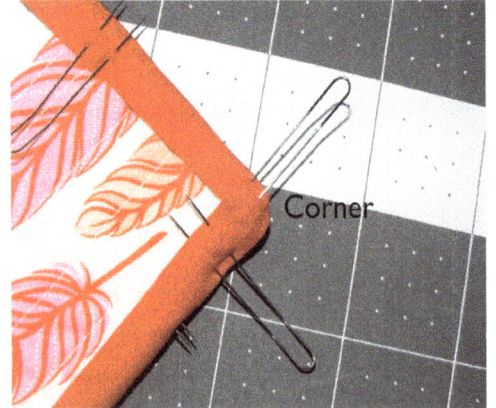

- Pin the binding level with the edge the rug, with the pin lying across the binding.

- Pin the binding all the way around the square. Use lots of pins so that you get your bias binding to lie nice and smooth.

- Fold the bias binding at the corners.

- When you reach the place where you started, measure ½ inch further and cut off the binding. Fold over ¼ inch and tuck the folded end *under the raw edge* at the start of the binding.

- Sew very close to the edge of the bias binding on the right side of your fabric. I usually sew about 1/8 inch from the edge of my bias binding. This way you will be sure to catch the back of the bias binding,

Ta-Da!!! Your mug rug is finished.

Binding Hint

- If you run out of binding before you get to the end of a quilt, you will have to join another piece to it.

- Stop pinning before you get to the end, Leave a few inches to work with.

- Place the new binding at right angle to the old piece right sides together and stitch corner to corner = left to right. Trim off the excess.

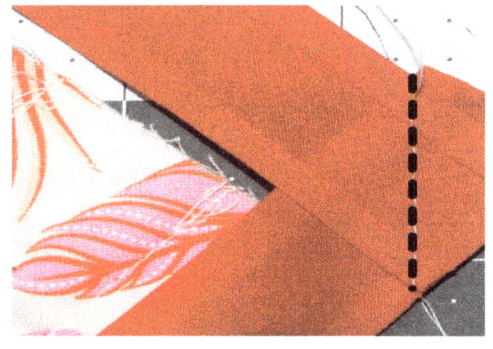

- Open the binding out and press the join. You will hardly see the seam. Continue binding.

The quilting skills you have mastered.

If you are a beginner, you have just made your first quilt. It may be a small one, but the skills you applied are exactly the same as those you would use in any quilt, no matter what size.

If you are an old hand, I hope you have picked up some tips to make quilting easier.

You have;

1. *Identified the tools you needed.*

2. *Chosen your fabric, batting, backing and bias binding and obtained enough to complete the project*

3. *Read and followed the instructions*

4. *Used the cutting mat, ruler and rotary cutter to cut out the pieces required for the quilt*

5. *Stitched the pieces together according to the pattern*

6. *Made the quilt sandwich*

7. *Quilted the sandwich using straight line quilting*

8. *Bound the quilt using bias binding*

Clever Cuts and Beaut Blocks

Short cuts to pieced patches

Half Square Triangle Short Method

Making Half Square Triangles (HST) usually means cutting two squares of different colours in half, then placing one of each colour triangle together face to face and sewing a ¼" seam down the long side. However there is an easier and faster way to create two HSTs.

Instructions

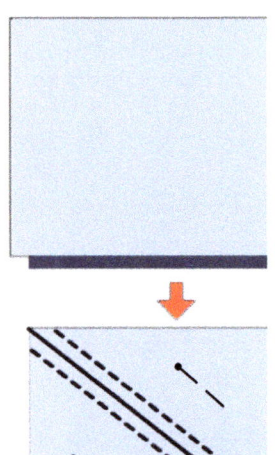

1. Cut two squares of equal size, one of each of your chosen colours.

2. Place one on top of the other right sides together.
3. Pin to secure them while you cut.

4. Draw a line diagonally from top right corner to bottom left corner.

5. Draw another line ¼" either side of that line.

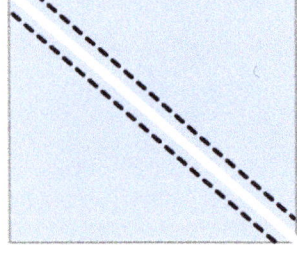

6. Take them to the sewing machine and sew down each ¼" line.

7. Cut along the middle diagonal line.

Open each of the two pieces and press the seam to the dark side.

Chain stitching

If you have more than 2 HST to make, for example, the Amish Star requires eight HSTs;

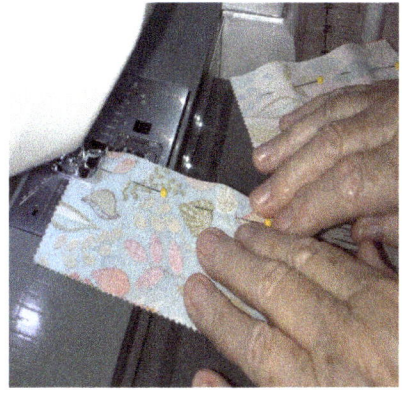

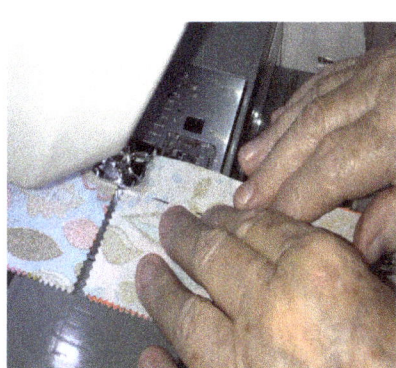

1. Before you do any sewing, mark and pin each of the sets of 2 squares. (For the Amish Star that would be four sets of 2 squares.) Then take them all to the sewing machine.

2. Sew down the outside lines of the first set but do not cute the threads after the second line.

3. Stitch 2-3 stitches and then slide the second set under the presser foot and sew both side lines, again sew 2-3 stitches at the end of the second line and slide the next set under the presser foot.

4. Repeat until all sets have been stitched.

5. Take them to your cutting board, snip the threads between each set and press.

This method allows you to cut all the HSTs you need in half the time.

A Modern Star

Using the Half Square Triangle

This is a 12 ½" unfinished block using only Half Square Triangles. It can also be used to create a Christmas Poinsettia by using 2 shades of red and substituting green for the other colour with no background white.

To make the purple block you will need these fabrics ;

- Three shades of a block colour;
  - Colour 1 - a dark shade
  - Colour 2 - a medium shade
  - Colour 3 - a light shade and
  - White

Cutting:

1. Cut four 3 ½" squares of Colour 1 fabric.
2. Cut two 3 ½" squares of Colour 2 fabric.
3. Cut two 3 ½" squares of Colour 3 fabric.
4. Cut eight 3 ½" squares of white fabric.

Instructions

5. Using the quick method of making HST squares. Match each white square with a colour square to make 2 HSTs.

You will end up with a total of 16 HSTs.

Following the colour numbers and direction of diagonals diagram below;

6. Join the squares in rows of four.
7. Join each row following the diagram from top to bottom.

Quarter Square Triangles

Quarter Square Triangles are much the same as HSTs. They look the same, but smaller. The only difference lies in cutting four at once, rather than 2, from 2 squares. There is a slight difference in the cutting, but it's an important one. We're cutting the two fabric squares twice diagonally. The danger of uneven cutting comes with the need to move the fabric 90⁰ to the right to make the second cut.

This is where the rule "**Move the mat, not the fabric!**" becomes paramount. If you have a rotating mat use it. If not, use your smallest mat and turn the mat 180⁰ to make the second cut. In my classes I often see quilters give the fabric a slight tug away from the ruler to make sure that it is cut. **Don't do this!** *That slight tug is the difference between even blocks and wonky blocks.*

If your rotary cutter blade is sharp, it will cut right through. If you are unsure, roll the cutter through the fabric two or three times, but keep your mitts off the material!!!!!

Let's cut

1. In the same manner as HSTs, place your two squares of equal size, one of each of your two colours, face to face (right sides together) on your cutting board.

2. Pin them together.

3. Take the block to the machine and stitch a ¼" seam all around the edge of the squares.

4. Take the sewn squares to the cutting board and draw diagonal lines from corner to corner.

5. With your rotary cutter, cut along the diagonal lines. **Turn the mat, not the fabric!!!**

6. Open out the squares and press the seam to the dark side.

You have four Quarter Square Triangles

3-Patch Quarter Square Triangle
Method 1

A   B

For this example we'll use 5 ½" squares
You need;

- For A - 2 solid or patterned colour squares (different colour or pattern), and
- For B - 2 background squares.

Let's cut

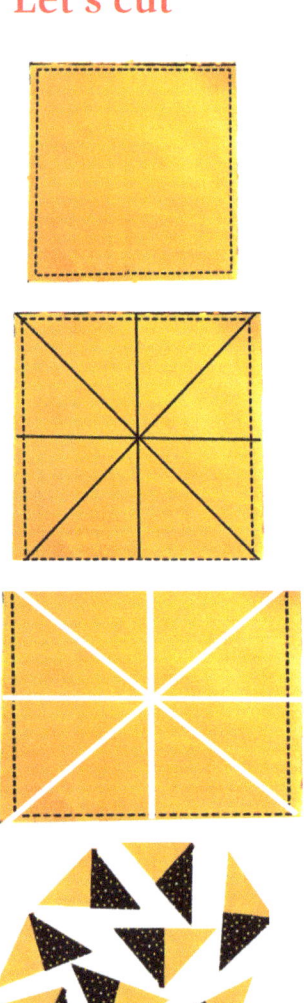

1. Place the A set of squares right sides together, matching the raw edges.

2. Sew **all around** the squares, ¼" from the edge on all sides.

3. Draw 2 diagonal lines corner to corner.

4. Mark the centre point of each side and rule a line down from the top to bottom centre mark and another from the left to the right centre points.

5. Cut along each line - ***turn the mat, not the fabric!***

6. Seperate the triangles and press to the dark side.

7. You now have 8 double triangles. Put them to one side.

110

8. Take the two 5 ½" contrasting squares.
9. Place them right sides together, lining them up to match the raw edges.
10. Mark two diagonal lines corner to corner.

11. Cut along the lines. You now have 8 quarter square triangles.

12. Take one half square triangle and one double triangle. Place them right sides together and stitch a ¼" seam down the longer side.

13. Open and press towards the background triangle.
14. Using the diagonal 45 degree line on your ruler, placed along the seam line, square the block to 3 inches.
15. Repeat with the other double ¼ square triangles and HSTs.

Et Voila!

Eight 3-Patch Quarter Square Triangles.

3-Patch Quarter Square Triangle
Method 2

A   B

You need;

- For A - 2 solid or patterned colour squares (different colour or pattern), and
- For B - 2 background squares.

Let's cut

1. Place the **A** set of squares right sides together, matching the raw edges.

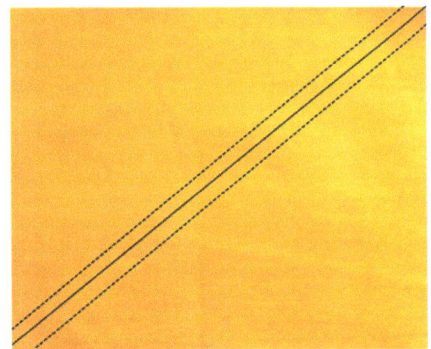

2. On the back of the lightest square, draw a diagonal line, right top corner to bottom left corner.

3. Draw 2 diagonal lines ¼" inch either side of the diagonal line.

4. Stitch down the two outside lines.

5. Cut along the centre line - **turn the mat, not the fabric!**

6. This creates 2 half square triangles. Press the seam open.

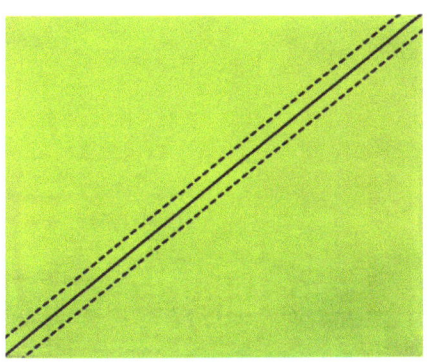

7. Take one of the HSTs and place right side up on your cutting board.

8. Take a one square from the B set of background squares and draw a diagonal line from corner to corner to corner on the wrong side.

9. Draw a line ¼" either side of that line.

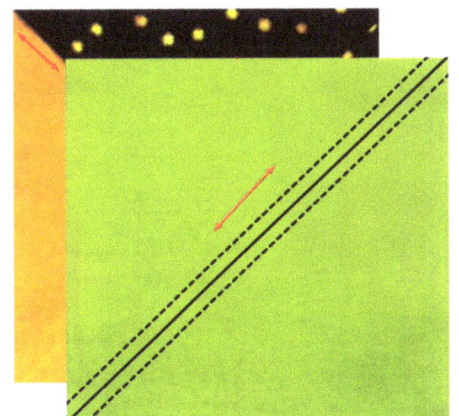

10. Place the background square right side down on top of the HST block so that the diagonal line you've drawn on the back goes *in the opposite direction of the HST diagonal line*.

11. Sew down the two outside line.

12. Cut along the centre line.

13. Open out the two blocks and press open.

Don't worry if the squares don't line up perfectly, you'll be trimming the units at the end.

14. Trim and square the block.

15. Repeat with the other HST and background squares

You now have two 3 Patch Quarter Triangle Squares

113

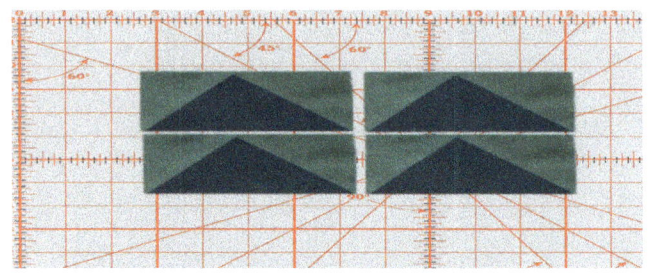

Flying Geese

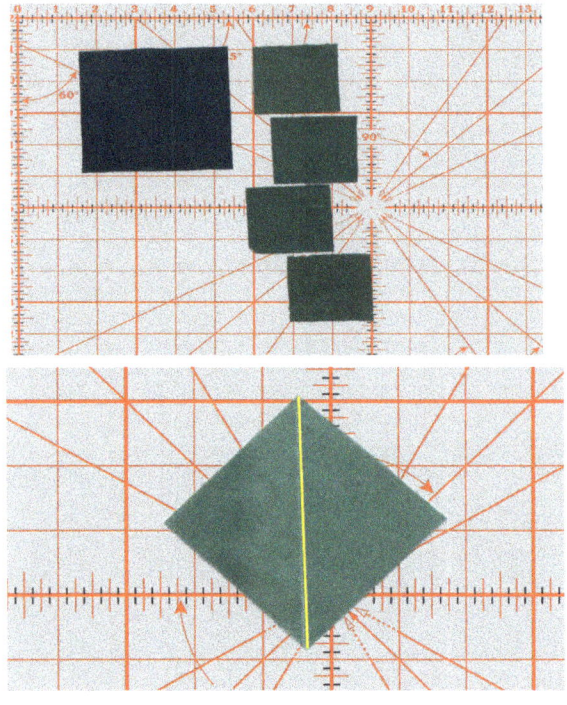

1. Cut 4 small squares and 1 large square for each set of 4 flying geese.

2. Take your 4 smaller blocks and with your marking pen and ruler draw a line right down the centre, as shown.

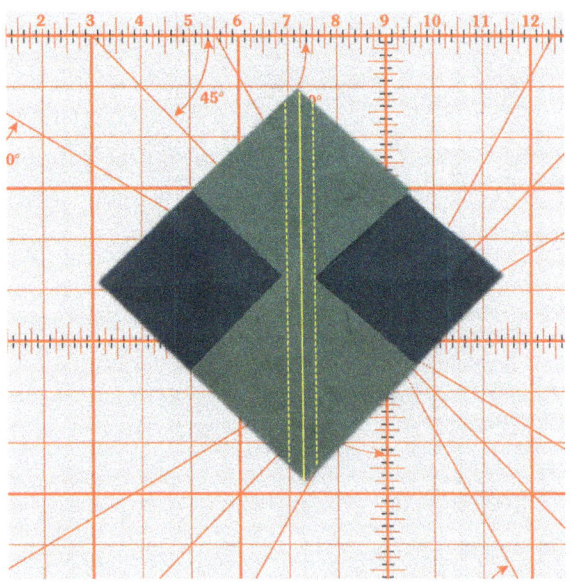

3. Now, take two of those smaller squares and place them RST (right sides together) with your larger square. They will overlap a tiny bit in the middle. Make sure you have them perfectly lined up on the corners. Use one pin on each square to hold them in place.

4. Sew ¼" lines on each side of the line you have drawn. The edge of the foot on most machines is ¼" so it's easy and fast to do. If your foot is not ¼ inch and you aren't sure, just use your quarter inch foot and you're good to go! Your block should now look like this.

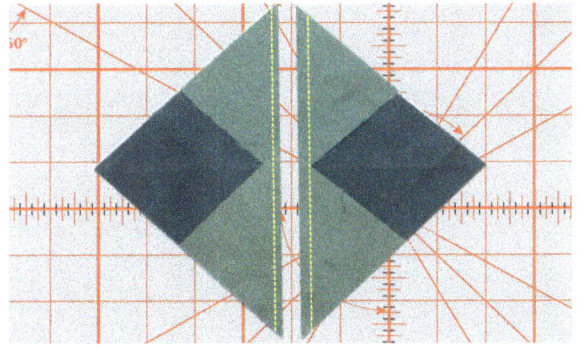

5. With your rotary cutter and ruler, cut directly down the centre on top of the line you drew.

6. Take your two pieces and press the seams to set them. Then, press the seam towards the two smaller triangles.

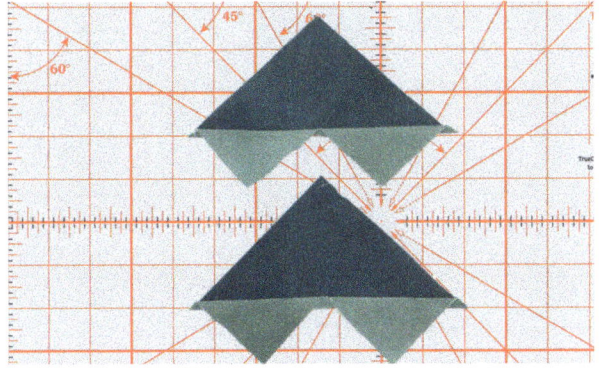

This picture shows the two blocks side by side. Note how the seam is pressing up towards the two smaller triangles.

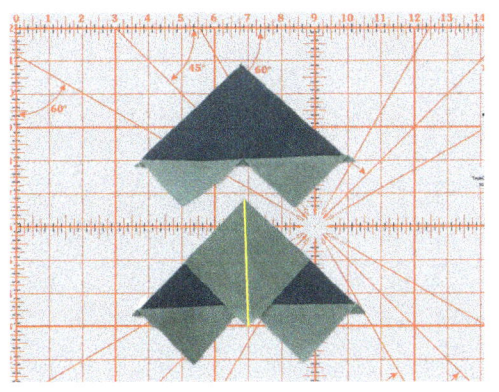

7. Take the remaining two smaller squares that you drew lines on earlier. Take one and lay it RST on the top corner of the larger triangle. Pin and then repeat with the other smaller square and triangle unit.

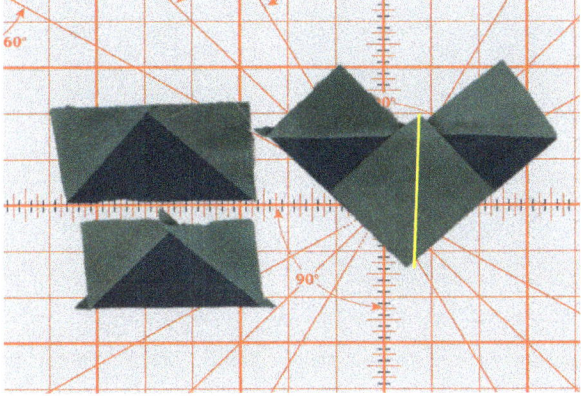

8. Just as before, sew ¼" on both sides of the drawn line. Start the first side by sewing from the top and then going down towards the smaller triangles. It is less bulk that way, the machine handles it better and it's flatter to sew the opposite direction for the second seam.

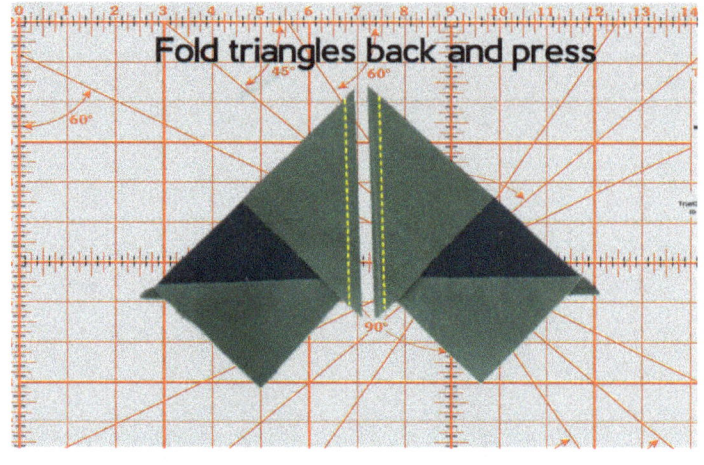

9. With your rotary cutter, cut down the line between the seams on both units and you'll end up with 4 smaller units (Flying Geese).

10. Once again, press the seams to set and then press the seam towards the smaller triangle.

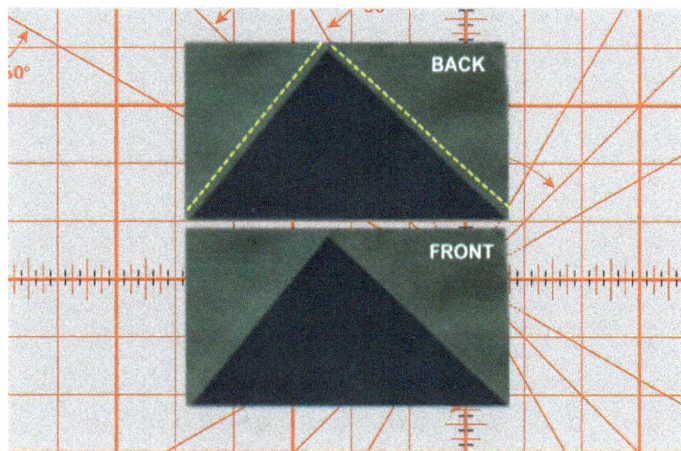

11. Back and Front picture.

   This illustrates how your pieces should now look.

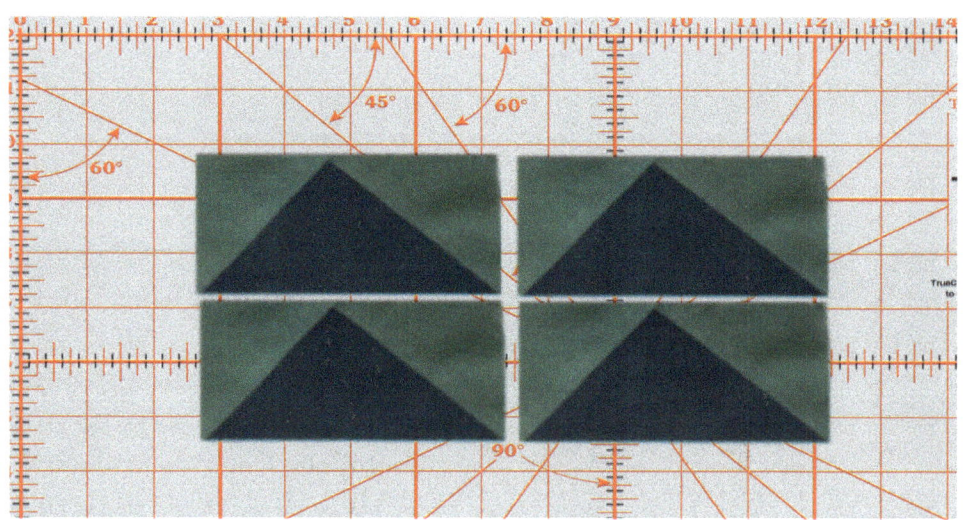

Snip off the tabs on the sides and you'll have with 4 perfect Flying Geese!

This chart gives you the sizes of the large and small squares you need to make different sized Flying Geese.

Note that both size squares are larger than the corresponding unfinished size of the sides of the Flying Geese patch. The large square is 1 inch longer than the long side, and the small square is ½ inch longer than the short side.

For example, look at the first line of measurements on the chart. The short side of the unfinished Flying Geese patch is 2 ½", so the small square size is 3 inches. The long side of the patch is 4 ½ inches, so the large square is 5 ½".

This is to allow for ¼ inch seams when the pieces are sewn together.

Finished Size	Unfinished size	Large Squares	Small Squares
2"x4"	2 ½" x 4 ½"	5 ½"	3"
2 ½" x 5"	3" x 5 ½"	6 ½"	3 ½"
3"x 6"	3 ½" x 6 ½"	7 ½	4"
3 ½" x 7"	4" x 7 ½"	8 ½"	4 ½""
4"x 8"	4 ½" x 8 ½"	9 ½"	5"
5" x 10"	5 ½" x 10 ½"	11 ½"	6"

Martha Washington's Star

Uses the 3 Patch Quarter Square Triangle Method 2 and Flying Geese Components

The Martha Washington's Star quilt block is a variation of the Sawtooth star. The pinwheel in the middle gives it a fun twist. It is often found incorporated into patriotic quilt designs and pieced in red, white and blue fabrics. Fabrics may be plain block colours or small patterned fabrics, e.g. dots, tiny flowers, small stars.

If using a very high contrast , e.g. red. bright orange, green, you can get away with a black background.

Cutting

Background fabric (white, cream, pale grey)

- Three 4 ½" x 4 ½" squares for the centre block.
- One 7 ½" square
- Four 4" x 4" squares

Dark pattern print (Flying Geese - Usually royal blue)

- Four 4" x 4" squares

Bright Pattern Print (Centre block Usually red)

- One 4 ½" x 4 ½" square

Instructions

1. Using the **3 Patch Quarter Square Triangle Method 2, *(p. 112)*** the three background 4" x 4" squares and the one 4" x 4" bright square, make 4 QSTs and square them off to 3 ½"

2. Sew the four blocks together to make one centre pinwheel block. (6 ½" x 6 ½")

3. Using the no waste quick method (p.114) with your dark print 4" squares and background 7½" square to make four Flying Geese. (3 ½ x 6 ½)

4. Now sew two of the flying geese to the sides of the pinwheel block, as in the image shown.

5. Sew the remaining 4 " x 4" background squares to the ends of the remaining two flying geese.

6. Sew the three sections together to create the 12 ½"x 12 ½" Martha Washington's Star

7. The block is finished.

You're a Star!!!

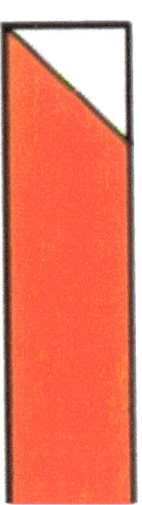

How put a triangle onto a rectangle.

This component is used in many different block designs, but particularly in stars and crosses.

You will need 2 fabrics for this practice activity.

- Use your main fabric for the strip and a contrast for the square.
- If the triangle at the top is to blend into the background, use the background fabric for the small square.

For this example I have used a shade of red for the rectangle and a background of white for the square.

Cutting

- Cut a strip 2" x 6 ½" in your
- Cut a 2" square from your background or contrasting fabric.

Instructions

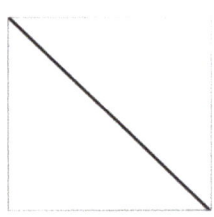

1. Draw a diagonal line on wrong side of the 2" square.

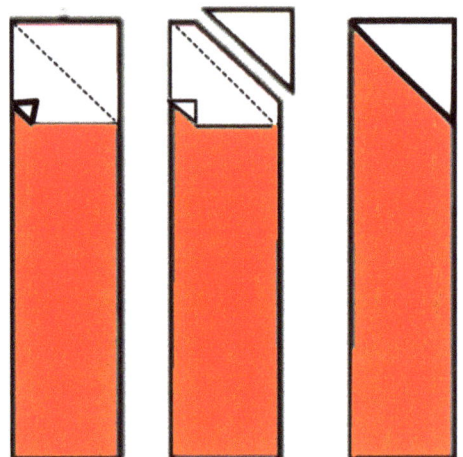

2. Place the marked square on the 2" x 6 ½" strip, right sides together. Line up the raw edges.

3. Stitch on the drawn line.

4. Trim away and discard the excess fabric

5. Open and press to make the pieced strip.

120

Sawtooth Block

Using the strip with triangle at the end. This block is formed by creating strips of dark, medium and light tones of the same base colour, tipped with a triangle of the background colour. It's a great block for using up leftovers from a completed quilt.

Cutting

White print
- Four strips 2″ x 6 ½″
- Twelve squares 2″ x 2″

Dark print
- Four strips 2″ x 6 ½″
- Four squares 2″ x 2″

Light print
- Four strips 2″ x 6 ½″

Medium print
- Four strips 2″ x 6 ½″

Assembling

1. Using the strips and squares you have cut, create;
   - Four white strips with a dark end triangle.
   - Four of each colour strip with a white end triangle.

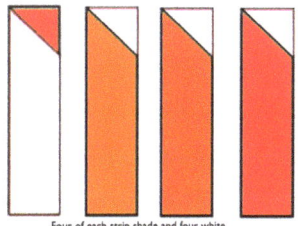

2. Sew one of each strip together using this image as a guide.
3. Repeat with the strips that are left until you have 4 identical squares.
4. Using the diagrams below as a guide, create two rows of 2 squares.
5. Sew the rows together to form the finished block, turning the squares to match the diagram.

Step 4

Make Rows

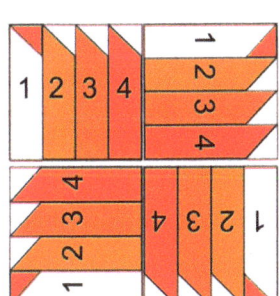

Step 4

Rows Joined

121

Cutting "One Way" Trapezoids

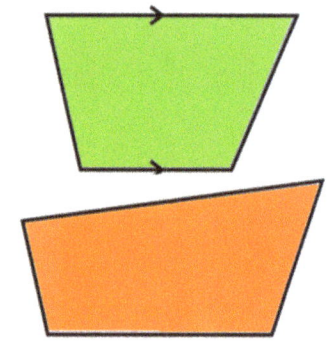

According to the Oxford Dictionary, a trapezoid is;

"a flat shape with four straight sides, one pair of opposite sides being parallel (= the same distance apart at every point) and the other pair not parallel"

A square can never be a trapezoid as it has all sides and angles equal. In quilting, trapezoid shapes are usually strips or rectangles with a 30, 45, or 60 degree angle cut at one or both ends,

Cutting a trapezoid piece is easy if you have a ruler that has 30, 45 and 60 degree lines marked across the ruler from one corner. If you don't have these lines, look at your cutting mat and see if they are there. A word of warning, if your angled line needs to run in a certain direction, e.g. Top left side to lower right side, make sure when you cut that you have your fabric with the side up that will give you the correct shape. If you are cutting more than one at a time, all pieces must be the same way up - all right side up, or all wrong side up, otherwise every second piece will be wasted.

Here is a practice trapezoid piece for you to try.

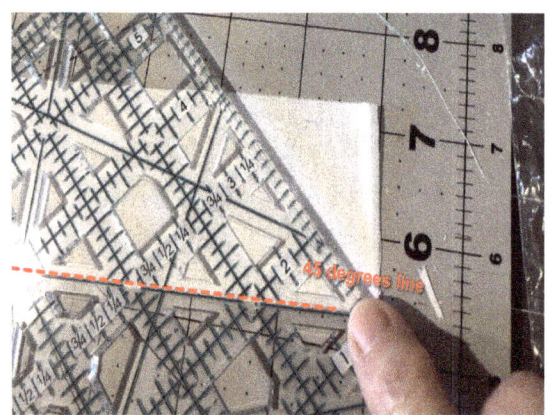

FOLLOW THE INSTRUCTIONS EXACTLY.

You need a 2 ½ " x 6" strip - 6" (a piece of jelly roll will do).

To turn it into a 45 degree trapezoid strip using your RULER;

1. Place rectangle/strip on your cutting mat.

2. Place the 45 degree line on the ruler on the long side of the rectangle as shown.

3. Using the 45 degree angle line on the ruler, cut off right corner.

To turn it into a 45 degree trapezoid strip using your mat;

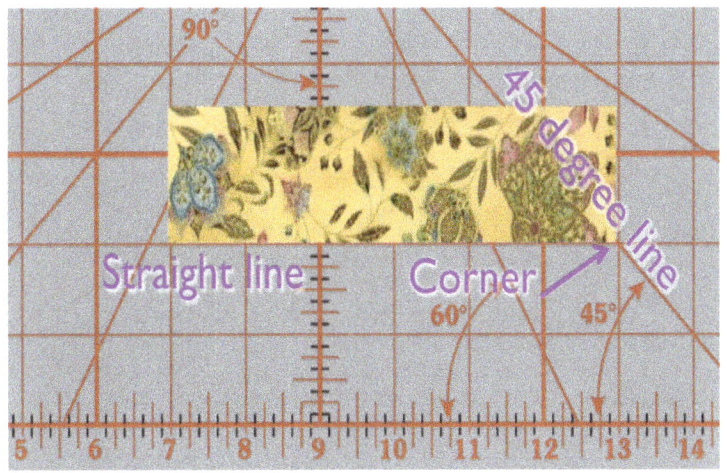

1. Place rectangle/strip on your cutting mat.

2. Line it up with a horizontal straight line.

3. Place the bottom corner of the rectangle on the mat's 45 degree line as shown.

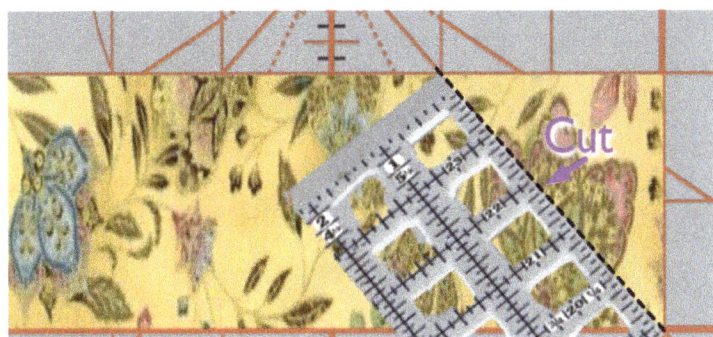

4. Place your ruler over the fabric lining it up with the 45 degree line on the mat.

5. Cut off the corner triangle.

To cut 30 degree or 60 degree angles, the same method can be applied, using the corresponding angle line on either your ruler or cutting mat.

A word about cutting mats and angle lines.

Most quality cutting mats have angle lines drawn on them. If yours does not, and you are considering replacing it with one that does, or simply replacing an old worn out mat, look for clarity, stability and multi-purpose use.

My favourites (currently available) are;

- For rotating mats - Fiskars 7" and 12" rotating mats - wish they had a larger one.

- For general cutting (on the basis of clarity and the helpful, non-verbal, visual information) Grace Company's cutting mats (3 sizes) - wish they had a rotating mat.

See the section on cutting mats for further information on choosing and caring for your cutting mat.

The following block looks very complex, but don't be fooled. If you have practiced quarter square triangles and trapezoid cutting, it's a doddle. It's a favourite in my Beginner's classes.

Double Pinwheel Block

This is such a great block to use. Tricky is the right word for the Double Pinwheel, but in a good way. If you know the right tricks it's easy-peasy. Look carefully at it and you'll see quarter square triangles, half trapezoid rectangles and squares. So give it a go!

You will need

1. Two contrasting fabrics plain or small pattern. A. For large blades B. For middle square

2. One striped fabric (the same tone as A) S for the striped blades.

3. A Neutral background fabric C.
   I recommend strong primary colours and a white or black background to make the most impact.

Cutting

Piece A

1. Cut two squares 5 ⅜″ from fabric Colour A.
2. Cut in half once diagonally to make four Half Square Triangles.

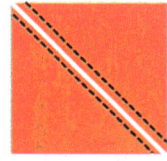

Piece B

1. Cut one square 4 ¾″ from Colour B.
2. Use the quick cut method to make four triangles.

Stripe - Piece S

1. Cut four rectangles 2 ¼″ x 5 ⅛″.
2. Cut into "one-way" half trapezoids

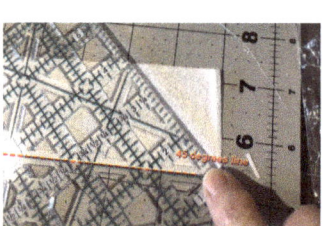

Piece D

1. Cut four rectangles 2″ x 6 ⅞″.
2. Cut into "one-way" half trapezoids

Piece E

1. Cut one square 7 ¼
2. Again, use the quick cut method to make four triangles.

124

Assembling

1. Stitch together pieces A – E as shown in Diagram II to make sub-unit.

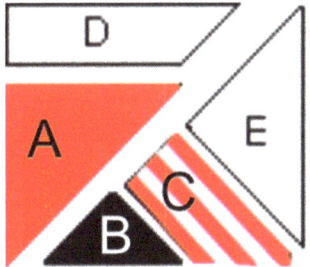  

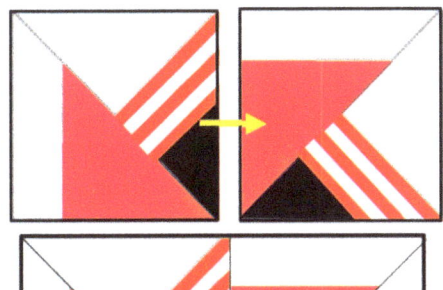

2. Sew 2 rows of 2 sub-units each.

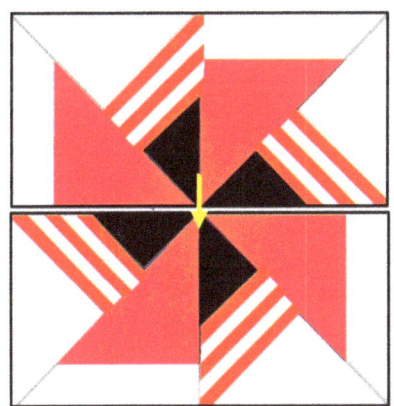

3. Sew rows together to make Double Pinwheel Block.

Change the colours and background to jump start your creativity !

125

A word about squaring up blocks

One of the skills that discombobulates my learners is squaring up a block or component once it's finished. Here's a step-by step that I hope will make it clearer and easier.

If you have cut the pattern to it's instructions, strictly and carefully it should be square, right? No, not necessarily right! If you have triangles in the block, they may have stretched on the bias. If you have ironed and not pressed your seams, it may be out of shape. You need to check that your block is truly square and is the correct size.

Once you have completed sewing the block and have trimmed off any "tails", it's time to make sure that your block is truly square.

There are two ways to do this;

- Using your square ruler
- Using your mat

The square ruler method

1. Place your block on the cutting mat.

2. Find the top corner of your ruler, where the 45° line starts and the numbers run to left to right from 1.

3. Place the corner of the ruler on the top left hand corner of the block and line up the 45° line to pass through the bottom right hand corner.

Let's say your block should be 12 ½ inches square, The sides of the triangle should line up all around with 12 ½ inches on the ruler. If so, you're all good and can start on the next block. If not, your block is not square and if you don't do something about it, your quilt will be wonky.

1. To square up turn the cutting mat **and the ruler** so that the wonky side is on the right (for left -handed quilters it should be on the left) with the start of the 45 degree line in the top right corner of the square.

2. Adjust the ruler so that the 45 degree angle line passes through the bottom left hand corner.

3. If there is any part of the fabric poking out from under the edge of the ruler, trim it off.

4. Repeat Step 1. If any side is out of line, repeat step 2.

The cutting mat method

This method can be used when there is not a 45 degree angle line on your ruler or your cutting mat. We'll assume this is a 5 ½" block.

Keep in mind half of 5 ½ is 2 ¾ .

1. Place your block on the cutting mat and a strong pin in the centre of your block. (A drawing pin works if you don't push it into the mat too far.)

2. Place the centre of you block at the centre point of your mat. Most mats that have angle lines have a point where they all cross - this is the centre point.

3. Pin the centre of the block to the centre of the mat.

4. Turn the block until one side is lined up with a horizontal line on the mat.

5. Take your ruler, line it up with the vertical line that is 2 ¾" away from the centre of the mat on the right. The edge of the block should line up with the ruler. If not, trim any excess.

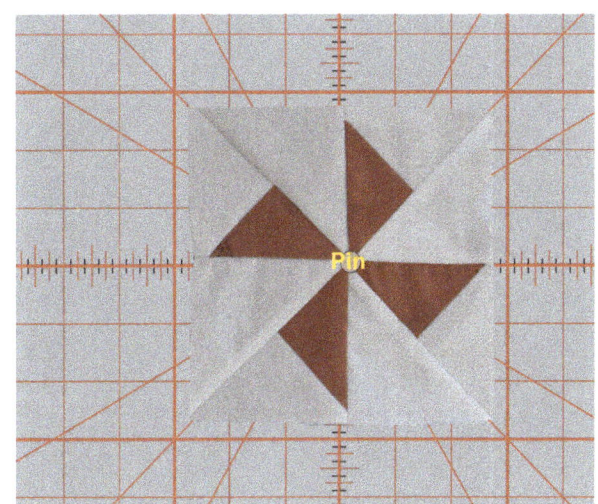

6. Remove the ruler and carefully turn the block to the right.

7. Repeat step 5. Repeat step 5 until all four sides have been trimmed when necessary. Take the pin from the block.

8. If you have a square ruler, place your ruler diagonally on the block, corner in the top left corner. It should line up exactly with the top and side. Repeat with the bottom right corner. If it lines up, you're all good. Well done.

9. If you don't have a square ruler, place the 5 ½" square block in the top left hand corner of the mat, lining up the top side with the top horizontal line and the bottom horizontal with the 0" and 5 ½" vertical lines. If the block lines up exactly on all sides, and are straight you're all good. Well done! Of not, trim the sides to straight and square.

Beaut Blocks

Block 1 - Simple Four Patch

You will need:

- Background fabric
- Block colour or patterned fabric

Instructions;

1. Sew 4 squares of the same size together using ¼ seam. (I use 5" squares)

2. Press the seams open.

A quilt made from 4 square patches might look like this.

The block is complete. However, we can use this block to have some fun.

Block 2 - Disappearing 4 Patch

You will need 1 simple four patch block.

Instructions:

1. Take the 4 patch block and place it face up on your cutting board.

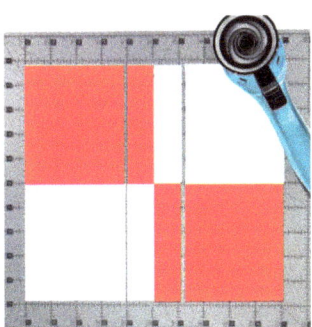

2. Start by cutting the block, 1" from the centre seam on 2 sides.

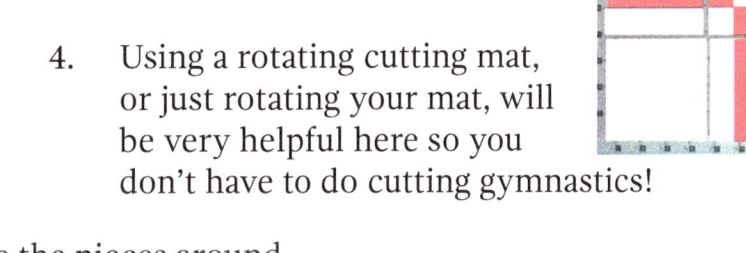

3. Then cut the other 2 sides.

4. Using a rotating cutting mat, or just rotating your mat, will be very helpful here so you don't have to do cutting gymnastics!

Move the pieces around

5. Rotate the centre block 90 degrees to the right to swap the corner squares.

6. *The long skinny pieces don't move!*

7. Sew it back together

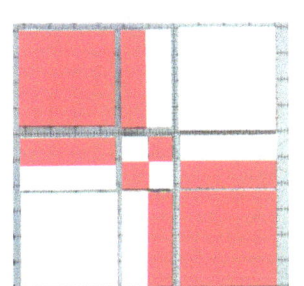

Ta-dah!

Block 3 - Disappearing 9 Patch

You will need;

- Three fabrics each a different colour/pattern
- One background fabric
- 5" charm squares are fine.

Instructions

1. Make a block of 9 patches of three rows of three equal squares following the diagram to the left. Make sure that the background squares are placed in the middle of the top, bottom and sides of the block. Whatever colour is in the middle will end up in all four of the final block-units. It doesn't matter where you put the others, they will be cut apart from each other in the next step.

2. Cut the block down the middle in both directions. You now have a parent block of 4 component blocks. There is a large square in the top and bottom corners.

3. Turn the top right block 180 degrees to the right so that the large square is in the centre

4. Turn the bottom left block 180 degrees so that the large square is in the centre You will have re-arranged the blocks to look as shown.

5. Sew the two top blocks together and do the same with the bottom blocks.

6. Sew the top row to the bottom row.

Ta-Dah - it's done!

Double Disappearing 9 Patch.
Make a **Double** Disappearing 9 Patch

You will need:

1. 9 small (5") squares
   - 5 mixed colours and/or patterns,
   - 4 background
2. 5 big (7") squares
   - 1 block colour and
   - 4 background colour

Instructions

1. Make a nine patch block. Whatever colour is in the middle will end up in all four of the final block-units.

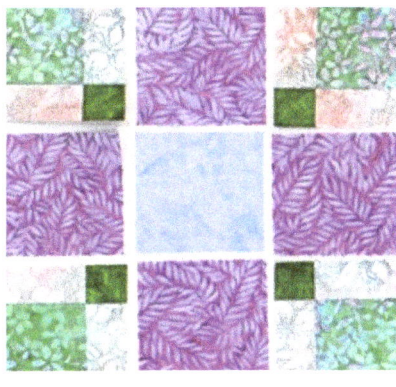

2. Cut the block down the middle in both direction Spread the blocks out, keeping their orientation to the centre.

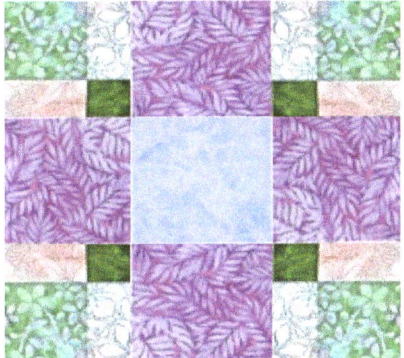

3. Use the larger squares to make a new disappearing nine patch block

4. Cut that block down the middle in both directions.

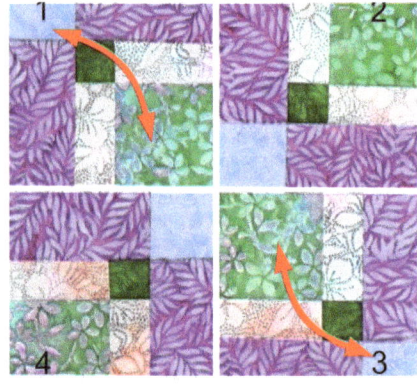

5. Rearrange the blocks

- Turn Block 1 180 degrees to the right so that the largest square is in the centre.
- Turn Block 3 180 degrees to the left so that the largest square is in the centre.

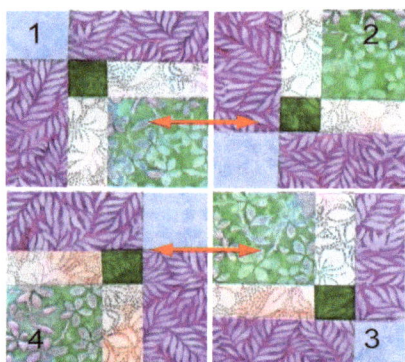

6. Stitch Blocks 1 and 2 together to form the top row.

7. Stitch Blocks 3 and 4 together to form the bottom row.

8. Stitch the top row to the bottom row.

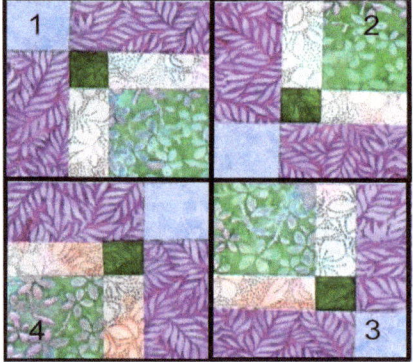

Whoopee! Your block is complete.

In case you want to start with different sizes for your beginning patches, you can use this formula for other sizes of the Double Disappearing 9 Patch.

Be warned - it's tricky!

Formula:

If ...

- X = size of small blocks **and**
- Y = size large blocks **and**
- Z = size of Unfinished block
- Y = 1.5 times X - ½"
- Z = 3 x Y - 2"

> **In our block**
>   **Small block is 5"**
>   **Therefore x = 5"**
>
> **Y= 1.5 x 5" = 7 - ½" = 7 "**
> **Therefore Large block is 7"**
>
> **Z = 3 x 7" = 21" - 2" = 19"**
>
> **Therefore our unfinished block is 19" square and the finished block will be 18 ½" square**

The problem is the small measurements can get VERY small - right down to 1/8" and less. Some blocks are quite easy. For example, the size of the squares to cut for a 10" unfinished block (9 ½" unfinished) are - small squares: 3" - big squares: 4".

Try it by all means, it's a fun math puzzle.

Sad to say, a 12 ½ inch block is impossible.

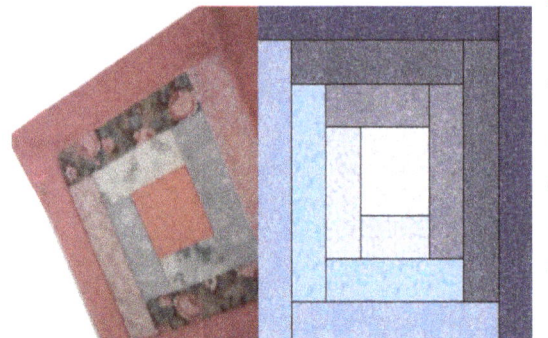

Block 4 - Log Cabin

The Log Cabin block can be made in mixed colours using fabric strips of varying matching shades, or in two tones. Either way, it's a great method of using up left over fabric or Jelly roll strips.

You will need;

- 1 block colour (a single hue or toning shades of the same hue) for the left half of the block.
- 3 contrasting fabrics, patterned or block, for the right half.
- 1 fabric for the centre square, contrasting with the others, so that it stands out a little.
- For the outer row of 'logs' use the same fabric from number 1, giving a border to the block.
- Trim as you go, squaring up each round.
- All seams are ¼ inch.
- This block is 10 ½ inches square.

Cutting Instructions

1. Cut 2 ½" x 12 ½" strips of each colour. Cut each strip in half. (6 ½" strips)
2. Lay out your strips side by side and check your design. When you are happy with it, mark the back of each strip with its number according to this diagram.
3. Plain colour strips should be numbered 3,4,7,8,11 and 12
4. Patterned/contrasting colour strips should be in pairs,
5. Pattern 1 – 1 and 2
6. Pattern 2 - 5 and 6
7. Pattern 3 – 9 and 10
8. Cut 1 x 4 ½ inch square in a contrasting plain or patterned colour.

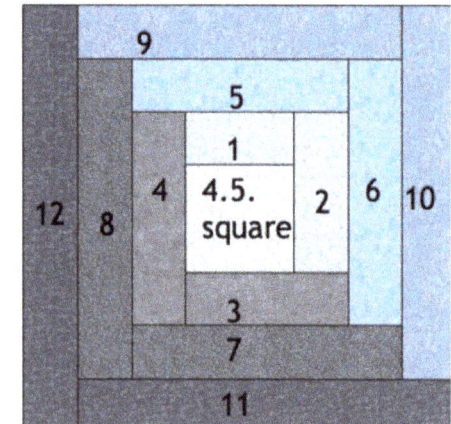

Piecing the Block

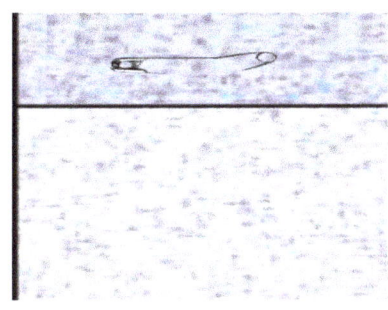

1. Take the centre square and strip 1.
2. Sew right sides together (RST).
3. Press the seam away from the centre and trim strip 1 to exactly same length as the square.

4. Put a safety pin in the first 'log'- strip 1, to mark it as the starting strip, and turn the block 90 degrees to the left so that strip 1 is at the top.

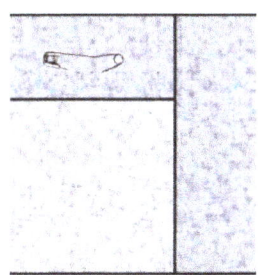

5. Attach strip 2 by sewing it down the right-hand side of the centre square & first strip.

6. Again, press the seams away from the centre and trim to bottom of the square.

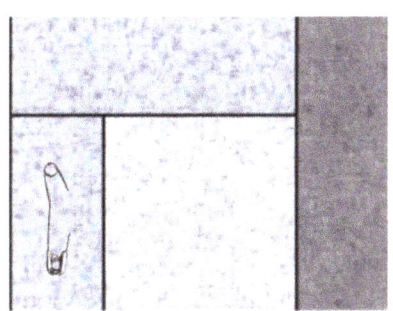

7. Turn your piece 90 degrees to the left so that strip 2 is at the top.

8. Take Strip 3 and, RST, sew it down the right-hand side of strip 2 and the centre square.

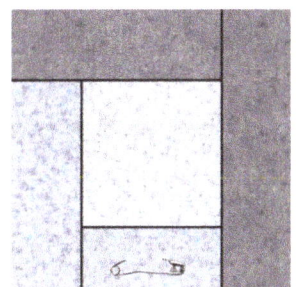

9. Turn your piece 90 degrees to the left so that strip 3 is at the top and strip 1 (with the pin is at the bottom.
10. Take Strip 4 and, RST, sew it down the right-hand side of strip 2, the centre square and the beginning of strip 1.

11. Turn your piece 90 degrees to the left so that strip 4 is at the top and strip 1 (with the pin) is at right.

12. Your first round is complete, square it up and trim if necessary. Leave the pin in piece 1 - it reminds you that you are about to start a new round.

Continue to work rows around the square following the pictures. Check at each start of a round that the block is square and seams are pressed away from the centre.

Piece 5

Piece 6

Piece 7

Piece 8

Piece 9

Piece 10

Piece 11

Piece 12 Your Log cabin block is done!

Woo-hoo! You did it!

Many quilters have used this block to make beautiful quilts.

Now, let your creativity go wild! You don't need to stick to block colours. Different patterned strips, contrasting coloured strips and a light side that vanishes into the background can be SO effective.

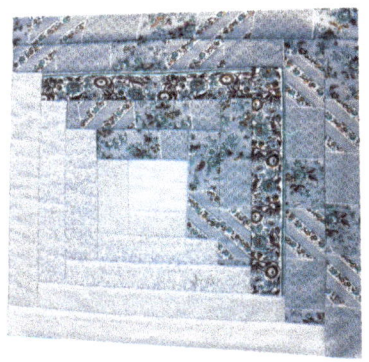

Block 5 - The Manx Quilt

The Manx Roof Block looks exactly like a Log Cabin block. It is, but the variation makes it even easier to master.

Manx quilting is one of the earliest forms of quilting in the Western world. The Manx log cabin block is fun to make, and you don't need anything but your hands. Everything is measured by your finger and thumb lengths.

You tear the fabric, and fold and stitch by hand. (Well, I admit, I cheat and use scissors to cut the strips to length,)

The Isle of Man is an island in the middle of the Irish Sea west of Northern England and Scotland. Its people are called the Manx or Mann. Their ancestors were Norse (Viking) and English. It is a self governed British Crown Dependency. Charles III is Lord of Mann and is re[resented by a Lieutenant Governor. A bit like Norfolk Island.

The earliest Manx quilt is said to have been made circa 1820. Almost everything on an island must be imported. At the beginning of the 19th Century this made life particularly expensive. The Manns wasted nothing, utilising as much material sourced from the island as possible. From this re-using of resources developed Manx quilting. No-one wanted to throw away old clothes and blankets. They could re-use empty flour, feed and sugar bags to create fresh blankets, floor coverings and household goods.

While we think of Quilt as You Go as a modern quilting method, the Manx beat us to it. Strips were an ideal use for scraps and they pieced them on a foundation backing in a quilt-as-you-go method. There is no batting in these quilts, making them lightweight and mostly decorative. Manx quilting was traditionally done with big hand-stitches, which would have been much simpler in the evening in darker homes, where lighting would have been expensive.

Let's have a go!

You need;

- Whatever scraps of fabric you have around.
- Your hands, a needle and thread, and maybe a pair of scissors.

Preparation:

1. Gather you fabric and decide which will be your backing and which will be the starting square. It is usually red, symbolising the heart of the home.
2. Tear you other fabrics into strips the length of the inside of your thumb. (That's about 2".)

Instructions

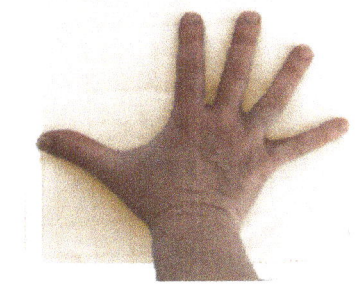

1. Measure your hand span. This is the measurement used to tear a square for you backing. As you will be using your finger and thumb for the other measurements, using your hand span keeps the block in proportion.

2. Using your handspan as the length of the sides, tear a square of backing fabric. The advantage of tearing the fabric is that woven fabric tears straight down the grain and straight across the grain, so your sides will be straight. (So will your strips when we get to them.)

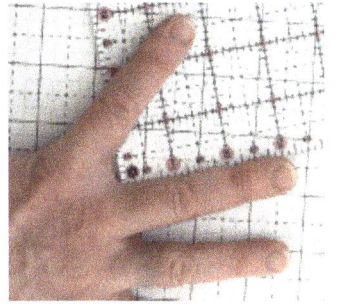

The length of the centre square comes from the length of the middle finger.

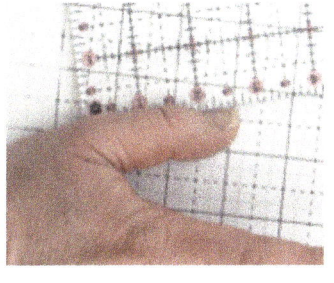

The width of the surrounding strips are measured from the length of the base of the thumb to the bottom of the thumbnail.

All fabric pieces are torn after an initial cut with a knife or by biting, but if you are a wuss you can use a ruler and rotary cutter.

3. "Mark" the backing fabric.
   - First, fold the backing square on both diagonals to mark an X in the fabric.

4. Using the X creases as a guide, centre the square in the middle of the foundation fabric.

5. Create a grid guide for placing the fabric "logs".
   - Fold the edge of the foundation square up to meet the edge of the centre square.
   - Finger press to crease at the fold.
   - Fold again, bringing the creased fold up to meet the edge of the square and crease the fabric at the new fold. You should have 3 even creased lines when you open it out.

6. Repeat steps on all four sides.

You should have 3 even creased lines on all four sides of the centre square.

These lines will be your guides.

7. Place the first strip at the top of the square, matching the raw edges. Stitch at a ¼" seam. (Start with a light coloured log, rather than a dark.)

8. Now fold the first 'log' strip back and line up the outside edge with the first crease in the foundation square. These creases, or fold lines, on the backing fabric are what creates the uniform-sized logs.

9. Pin the strip in place to keep it from slipping out of place before adding the next log..

Instead of folding the strip all the way back for a nice, flat open seam like we traditionally do in quilting, this will create about a ¼" pleat at each seam.

Rotate the foundation block clockwise 90 degrees, ready to add your next log.

10. Repeat the same step, adding another log, this time along the edge of both pieces. Exactly as you would with a Log Cabin block.

It's traditional to keep all of the logs the same width, but don't stress about the length of your logs. If the log is too long, trim it off with scissors after you have stitched it in place.

11. Fold the new log to the first crease on that side, rotate the block and prepare to repeat these steps to continue building your block.

12. As with a traditional log cabin block, always add the next strip above the end of the previous log.

    Stitch and fold each strip, rotate the block and repeat with the next strip. Continue to build the block, moving the pins to the outer strips as you go, until you have 4 strips on each side of the centre square.

13. On the last round, *stop stitching ¼" away from the edge of each strip*. You need to have a ¼" space right around the block to join the pieced blocks together.

The block should have 4 strips (or logs) on each side of the centre square.

Phew - all done!

Here's the finished block!

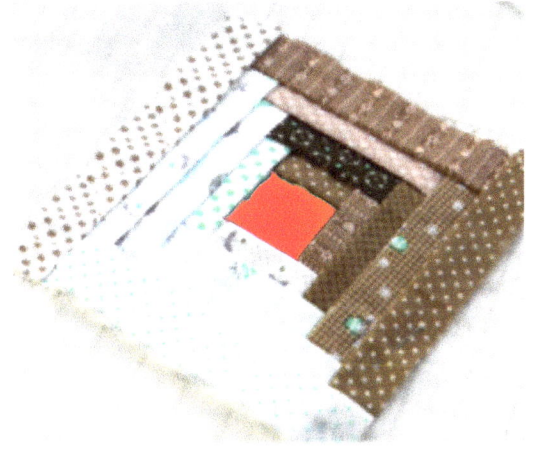

Block 6 - Martha Washington's Star
Traditional method.

The Martha Washington's Star quilt block is a variation of the Sawtooth star. The pinwheel in the middle gives it a fun twist. It is often found incorporated into patriotic quilt designs and pieced in red, white and blue fabrics. Fabrics may be plain block colours or small patterned fabrics, e.g. dots, tiny flowers, small stars. If using a very high contrast , e.g. red. bright orange, green, you can get away with a black background.

Cutting

Background fabric (white, cream, pale grey)

- One 7 ¼"x7 ¼" square cut into quarter square triangles (See QST in Block Components section.)

- Two 3 7/8" x3 7/8" squares

- Four 4 ¼" x 4 ¼" squares cut into quarter square triangles (See QST in Block Components section.)

- Four 3 ½ x 3 ½" squares

Dark pattern print (Usually royal blue)

- Four 3 7/8" x 3 7/8" squares

Bright Pattern Print (Usually red)

- One 4 ¼"x 4 ¼" square cut into quarter square triangles (See QST in Block Components section.)

Instructions

1. Sew the small bright triangles to the small background triangles as shown. You will need four of these pieces.

2. As shown in the image, sew a medium background triangle to the double quarter square piece you have just made. Make four of these.

3. Sew the four blocks together to to make one centre pinwheel block.

4. Use your dark print and background squares to make four Flying Geese. (See Flying Geese component)

5. Next sew two of the flying geese to the sides of the pinwheel of block as in the image shown.

6. Take the four 3 ½" x 3 ½" squares and sew them to the ends of the remaining two flying geese.
You should have of these strips.

7. Sew the three sections together to create an unfinished 12 ½"x 12 ½" Martha Washington's Star

8. The block is finished.

You're a Star!!!

Traditional Sawtooth Block

See the components section for the shortcut method.
Finished Block Size 12" x 12" Unfinished 12 ½" x 12 ½"

You will need four fabrics, three shades of a primary colour, solid or pattern or both and white as a background.

Cutting

White print
- Four strips 2" x 6 ½"
- Twelve squares 2" x 2"

Light print
- Four strips 2" x 6 ½"

Dark print
- Four strips 2" x 6 ½"
- Four squares 2" x 2"

Medium print
- Four strips 2" x 6 ½"

Instructions

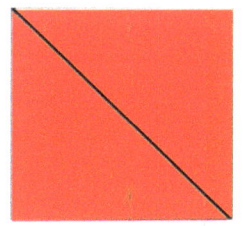

1. Draw a diagonal line on wrong side of dark 2" square.

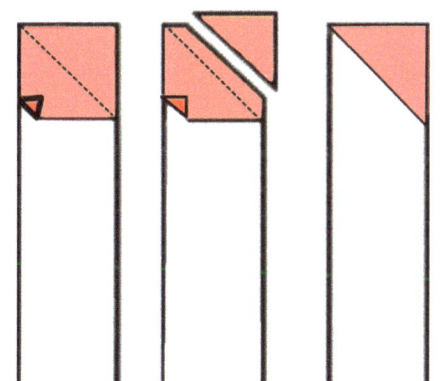

2. Place marked square on white print 2" x 6 ½" strip, right sides together. Line up the raw edges.
3. Stitch on drawn line.
4. Trim away and discard excess fabric.
5. Open and press to make pieced strip. Make three more.

145

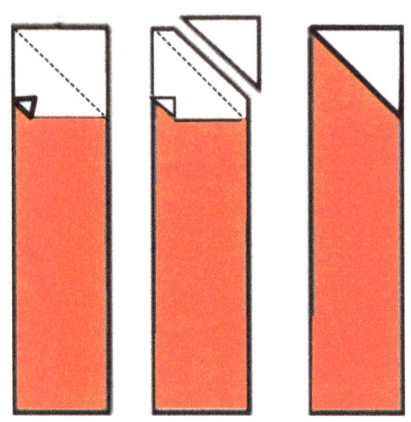

6. Using the strips and squares you have cut, create;
   - Four white strips with a dark end triangle.
   - Four of each colour strip with a white end triangle.
7. Sew one of each strip together using this image as a guide.

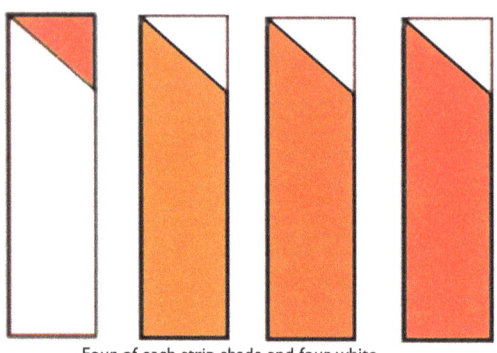

Four of each strip shade and four white

8. Repeat with the strips that are left until you have 4 identical squares.

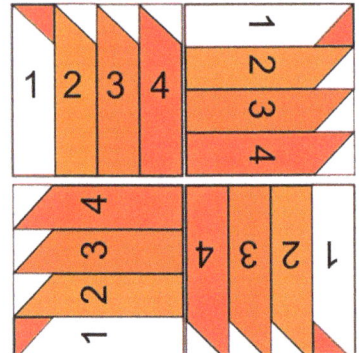

9. Using the diagrams as a guide, create two rows of 2 squares.

10. Sew the rows together to form the finished block, turning the squares to match the diagram.

Easy as 1 2 3!

What is QAYG?

QAYG stands for "Quilt As You Go", a recognised method for creating a quilt from a set of blocks that you have individually pieced, sandwiched and quilted.

It is hard to machine quilt a large project on a domestic sewing machine. Constantly pushing, pulling, and trying to keep track of a big rolled up quilt through a regular sized sewing machine is a stretch for any quilter, never mind us old chooks! We would all love to have a beautiful long-armed sewing machine designed for quilting, but the chances of that can be remote if you are on a pension. But, hey! We can all wish! In the meantime, while we wait for our Fairy Godmother to appear, Quilt As You Go is our perfect solution.

To QAYG, take each block, batting and backing, sandwich them together and quilt it. When you have finished all the blocks, join them together to complete your glorious quilt.

QAYG, step by step.

Step 1 - Plan

Solid planning is extremely important. You need to know which blocks you are going to use, how many blocks you will need and how much fabric to buy.

The last thing you want is to run out of fabric with two blocks to go - I know, I've done that. By the time I realised I was short half a metre of two fabrics, the design collection was discontinued and I was up the creek without a paddle.

Before you start you must;

- Find or create a pattern you will use for your quilt.
- Work out what size the blocks will be.
- Find the right combination of colours and fabrics you want to use.
- Decide whether to use pre-cuts or yardage, or some of both.
- Work out the amount of fabric you will need for your quilt, including your backing fabric, batting and enough top fabric for the sashing strips.
- Acquire your fabric, batting and batting.

Step 2 - Make your blocks

Put the backing and batting to one side for now and concentrate on your blocks.

1. Cut and stitch together the tops for all the blocks.

2. Once your blocks are ready, lay them out and make sure you have them all and that they are correctly made and the right size.

3. Now get your backing fabric and batting ready.

   - Cut the backing about an ½ inch wider all around than the block
   - Cut the batting the size of the block.

4. Place the backing right side down on your cutting board.

5. Place the batting, centred, on top of the backing fabric.

6. Place the block *right side up* on top of the batting.

7. Pin the sandwich together ready for quilting

Quilt each block

Choose your favourite quilting method, for example;

- Straight line quilting
- Stitch in the ditch
- Free motion quilting

Step 4 - Cut and make your sashing

Sashing is the strip of fabric you use to join the blocks and rows together. It can be any width, from very narrow to whatever width you need. It is folded like bias binding and covers raw edges of blocks and rows where they are joined.

There are different styles of sashing strips, but for this exercise, we will use a plain sashing. You will need enough strips to join the blocks, the rows and the binding,

To calculate the number of strips for joining the blocks;

- Take the number of blocks in a row - say 4
- Calculate the number of strips in the row - 3
- Calculate the number of rows - say 5

If the blocks are 10 ½ inches square, each strip will be 10 ½ inches long.

Therefore you need 15 x 10 ½ " strips for the block sashing

To calculate the length of sashing strips needed to join the rows ;

- Take the number of rows in the quilt - say 5
- Calculate the number of joins - 4
- Calculate the length of each strip

As each block once joined is now 10" and there are 4 in a row with 2" sashing between each block, the length *should* be 46 inches **BUT** the first and last block are 10 ¼ inches (one side of each is not joined) so the length of each row sashing must be 46 ½"

Therefore you need 4 x 2 ½ inch strips, 46 ½ inches long for the row sashing.

To calculate the binding;

- The quilt is 47 ½ inches wide and 58 ½ inches long.

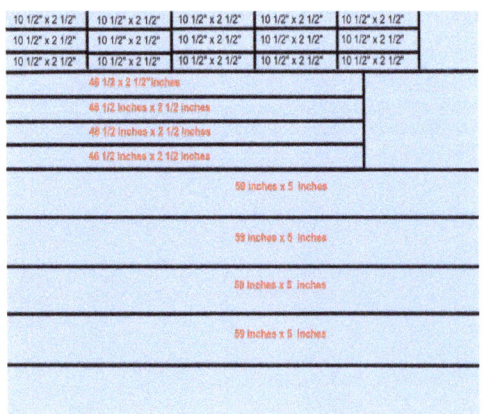

Therefore to bind all around the four sides of the quilt will take 212 inches of 5 inch binding. This does not have to be cut in a continuous strip, the binding can be pieced from shorter lengths.

How much fabric?

The WOF in Australia is 110 cm (43") or in USA 42" if you are using Australian metreage to buy, you will need to work out how best to get the most out of 110 cm wide.

A word about sashing

Making your own sashing using the fold and iron method can be tricky, particularly if you are making a long piece. To get an even, straight piece of binding, crisply folded and pressed so that the width when folded is the same all the way along requires concentration and a steady eye and hand. There are tools that will help you.. This is not a job for the breakfast bar or table. Before you can use any of the tools, you need a stable ironing board and an iron that you can use without steam.

Binding tools

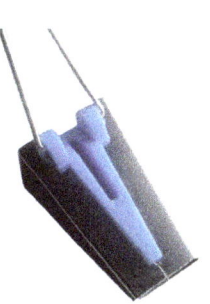

The first kind of tool has been around forever. Known as a bias binding tool, it comes in a number of sizes. Despite the name, your fabric for sashing is not cut on the bias, but the straight grain. The tool still works. For sashing, your strip of fabric needs to be twice the finished width of the sashing. For a 2" finished sashing your fabric must be 4" wide and you must use a 4" binding too..

Here's how it works.

1. For a 2" finished sashing, cut the sashing fabric 5" wide and make any joins necessary to make it the length you need. For example, for four 10 ½" long sashing pieces you will need the width of the 42" fabric.

2. Fold the starting end of the strip in half . Make a cut at an angle from the end of the fold diagonally to the two raw edges - only about 1 -2 cm from the end. Open the fabric out flat and you will have created a small "V" at the start of the sashing strip. Take your sashing tool and fabric to the ironing board. If you are right handed, your iron will be at the right end of the ironing board (the widest part). If you are left handed, your iron will be on the left.

3. Line up the fabric with the pointed end at the widest point of the board and the fabric laid face (right side) down along the board in a straight line to the narrow end.

4. Feed the pointed end of the fabric into the widest part of the tool and gently move it forward through the tool. It will come out of the narrow part of the tool folded.

I find I can start the fabric moving through the binding tool easily if I place the pointed blade of my stitch ripper into the space between the blades of the tool and into the start of the fabric. I can then ease it through the tool keeping the point in the middle and ensuring it comes out with even folds at the ironing end.

5. With your iron on the folded fabric, pull the tool towards the narrow end of the ironing board following it with your iron, holding the tool in place with the handle as you go.

6. As you work, stop and move the tool and fabric towards the wider end of the ironing until it is in a good position for you continue, allowing the already pressed fabric to dangle over the broad side towards the floor. When you reach the other end, your sashing will be folded and ready to use.

Pauline's Rogers Sashers

Another tool, which I find is easier to use, has more flexibility for use and is kinder to unsteady hands, is the Sasher that was invented by Pauline Rogers. Based in Toowoomba, Qld, Pauline is known in Australia as the "Quilt As You Go Lady", and has been for many years. It was from Pauline I discovered QAYG and her marvellous collection of sashers and templates for quilting.

The Sashers are made of a heat resistant material. The sasher does not melt or distort when the iron touches it. There are a large number of sashers for different widths and styles of sashing, including one made specifically for Jelly Roll strips, YAY!!!

BEWARE, there are copies of Pauline's invention available cheaply on the web but they melt and distort with the heat of an iron. You get what you pay for, and several quilters I know have thrown their money away on cheap fakes. Pauline's sashers have her name clearly marked in the plastic at the top of every sasher.

To make sashing with the tools;

1. Decide how wide a sashing you want to fold. Cut and join any sashing strips you want to fold and choose the correct sasher to give you the width you need. Remember - your strip needs to be twice the finished width of the sashing.

2. Take the sasher and fabric strip to the ironing board.

3. Line up the fabric right side down along the ironing board with the start closest to the iron and the wide end of the board.

4. Fold the strip in half, only for about 8 cm, matching the raw edges and press.

5. Open up the fold and fold the two sides over to meet the centre crease. Press for about 8cm making sure that the sides are lined up with the centre crease.

6. With the handle of the sasher towards you, pass the 8 cm of folded strip- folded sides on the top, up through the slot in the sasher, over the middle bar and down through the other slot.

7. Using forked pins, pin the end to the iron board as close to the wide end of the ironing board as possible.

8. Place the iron between the pins and the sasher and using the handle to guide, use the edge of the iron to slide the sasher along the strip.

   It will fold the fabric as it goes, giving you an crisp, straight, even width of sashing.

9. As you reach the length of the ironing board, take the iron off the fabric, and place it on its ironing board stand. Unpin the start of the strip, lift the strip and move the strip and sasher together to the wide end of the board, allowing the finished section to dangle over the end.

10. Pin the fabric to the board a cm or two on the starting side of the strip, in front of the sasher. Leave nough room between the pins and the sasher for the iron. Make sure the sasher is straight on the end of the folded part of the strip.

11. Again use the handle to guide it as you repeat the pressing of the unfinished part of the sashing. Repeat the process until you have pushed the sasher past the end of the strip. Now cut the sashing into the different lengths you need.

I find Pauline's sashers by far the easiest way to create QAYG sashing, You'll find more creative ways to use them, and a wonderful guide to Quilt As You Go in Pauline's book, "Quilt As You Go With Pauline Rogers". Pauline also has a website and online store, http://www.pqw.com.au , where you can obtain the sashers, templates and other tools that she has produced. The website also has video tutorials on how to use the sashers as well as her QAYG techniques and advice.

It's well worth a visit - you'll go back again and again.

How to prepare your sashing

If you don't have sashing tools, go ahead and make your sashing by hand.

For our example quilt, if you laid out your cutting well, you would get all the sashing and binding out of 1.25 metres of fabric, cut on the straight grain.

10 1/2" x 2 1/2"	10 1/2" x 2 1/2"	10 1/2" x 2 1/2"	10 1/2" x 2 1/2"	10 1/2" x 2 1/2"
10 1/2" x 2 1/2"	10 1/2" x 2 1/2"	10 1/2" x 2 1/2"	10 1/2" x 2 1/2"	10 1/2" x 2 1/2"
10 1/2" x 2 1/2"	10 1/2" x 2 1/2"	10 1/2" x 2 1/2"	10 1/2" x 2 1/2"	10 1/2" x 2 1/2"

| 46 1/2 x 2 1/2" inches |
| 46 1/2 inches x 2 1/2 inches |
| 46 1/2 inches x 2 1/2 inches |
| 46 1/2 inches x 2 1/2 inches |

| 59 inches x 5 inches |
| 59 inches x 5 inches |
| 59 inches x 5 inches |
| 59 inches x 5 inches |

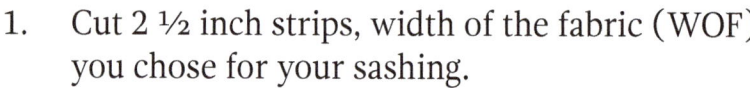

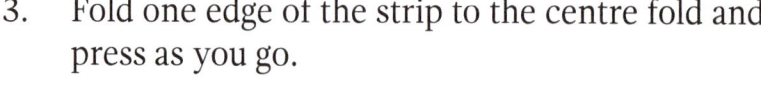

1. Cut 2 ½ inch strips, width of the fabric (WOF) you chose for your sashing.

2. Fold each strip in half longways and press.

3. Fold one edge of the strip to the centre fold and press as you go.

4. Repeat with the other edge.

5. Cut some of the strips into lengths the size of the side of the blocks, e.g. 10 1/2 inches.

Assemble the Quilt

Number the blocks

1. Lay out your quilted blocks in order and number them from the top, e.g.

   - Row 1 block 1. Row 1 block 2 and so on to the end of the top row.
   - Row 2 block 1. Row 2 block 2 and so on to the end of the next row

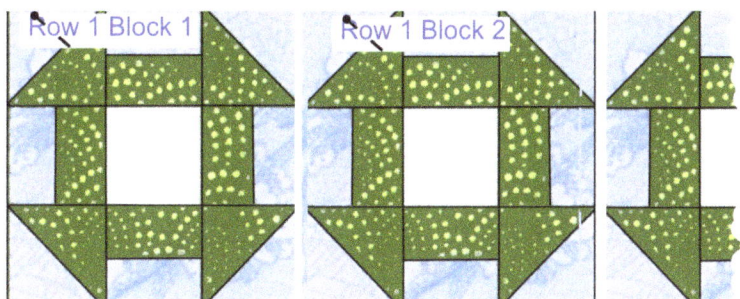

2. Number all the blocks to the end of the last row.

Join the rows

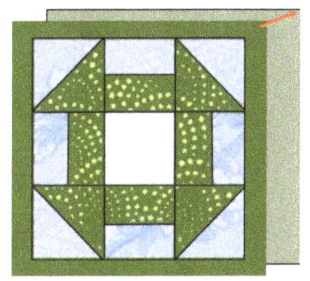

1. Place Your First Two Pieces.
   Take Row 1 block 1 and Row 1 block 2, matching the top and bottom of the blocks, and place them back to back.

2. Using a ¼ inch seam, sew the blocks together down the right hand side.

3. Open the two blocks and place them right side up on your cutting board.
   Work from one end of each row to the other.

4. Take one strip, place it right side up and folded edges down over the point at which the two blocks meet. Do not place the sashing over the ½" backing at the top and bottom of the blocks. You will use this to attach the rows together later on.

5. Carefully pin the strip in place keeping it straight along the joins.

Start Stitching

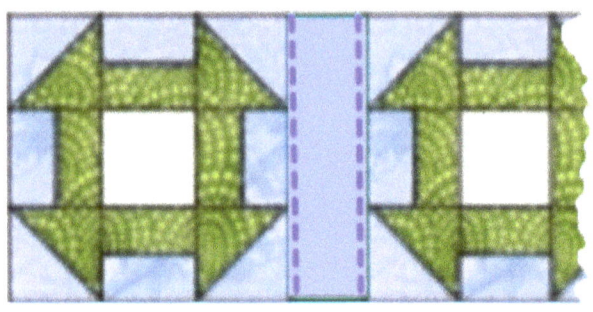

1. Start at the right hand edge of the strip, close to the folded edge (I place my needle in the right hand position) and begin stitching down the edge of the strip.

2. Turn the blocks and stitch the other side of the strip the same way.

3. Take Top Row Block 3 and join it to Block 2 the same way.

4. Repeat Steps 1-4 for each sashing strip until you finish the row.

5. Repeat the process for each row, joining the blocks together and sashing as above.

Join the rows.

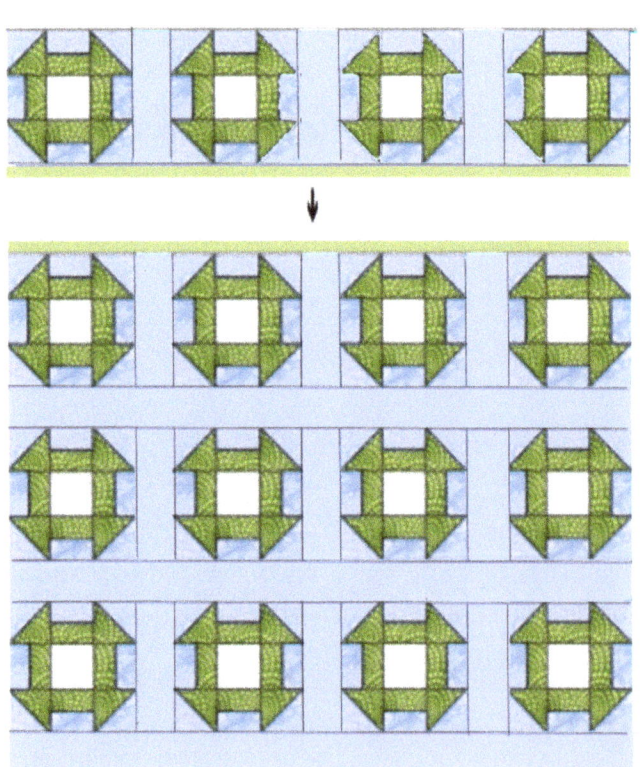

1. Take row 1 and row 2,

2. Lay row 1 right side up on your table.

3. Lay row 2 right side down on top of row 1.

4. Pin the bottom edges,

5. Stitch as close to the bottom of the blocks as possible.

6. Open the rows.

7. Sash the rows using the same process used to sash the blocks.

8. Row 2 to Row three using the same process, and so on until all the rows are joined.

9. Square up the quilt, trim off any excess sashing down the sides.

Once you've finished, the only thing left to do is the binding.

When you use this method, you're seaming your pieces together, and you're also quilting the back as you go along. The QAYD method is a great way to get a big project done in a much shorter amount of time.

There is a foolproof way of making sure that your strips are correctly placed and stay there when you stitch them, Roxanne Glue-Baste-It. I buy mine online.

By placing small dots of glue along each side of the join, then lining up your strip and pressing it onto the glue, you will be able to see that it is placed and centered correctly. Once it is, press the sashing in place. If not, you can remove it by pulling it away, re-place it and press again. You can then sew down one side and then the other without needing pins.

Roxanne glue washes out and does no harm to your machine when you sew through it. However, a word to the wise, choose the bottle with the needle point, not the tube with the comb at one end. My experience has been that the flat ends may leak when stored and floods while using it.

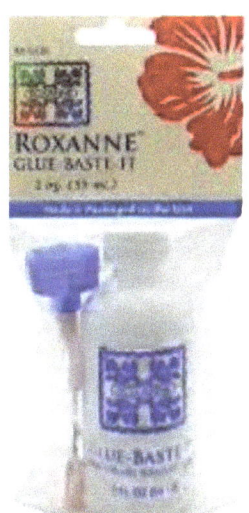

This double bed quilt was made using QAYG with sashing.

However, you don't always have to sash the blocks and rows.

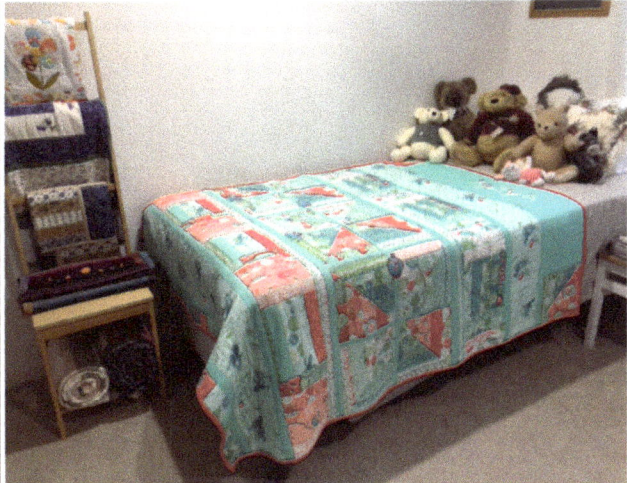

QAYG Variations

Joining blocks and rows without sashing

To join blocks without sashing, change the following steps;

1. When cutting the batting, make it ½ inch smaller than the block.

Join Block 1 to Block 2

2. Lay block 1 face down on the table.

3. Place Block 2 on top of block 1 face up.

4. Stitch ¼" seam down the right side

5. Open up the blocks

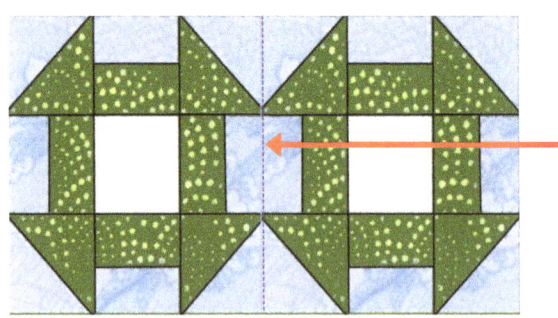

6. Fold the ¼ inch overhang on block 1 over the ¼ inch overhang on block 2 and hand stitch it in place. (You can use your Roxanne Glue to hold everything in place before you stitch.) Alternatively, you can machine stitch the edge as you would the sashing - it's a personal choice.

7. Continue joining the blocks to the end of the row.

8. To join the rows, use the same process, joining first the back ¼ inch overhang, and then the front as in step 3.

Different kinds of sashing

Sashing is strips of fabric joining QAYG blocks and rows. Not all sashings are a simple strip of colour or patterned fabric. You will find many different kinds of sashing in Pauline Rogers' "Quilt As You Go with Pauline Rogers" available from her website.

Cornerstone

This is just one sashing variation, which has squares at the corners of the blocks. These are known as cornerstones.

Cornerstones have sides that match the width of your sashing. If you cut sashing strips 5" inches wide your cornerstones should be 5" square.

How Many Sashing Strips and Cornerstones Are Needed?

- How many blocks will there be in each row?
- How many rows will the quilt have?
- How wide will the sashing be?

Work out the number of times the sashing strips between rows meet the sashing strips between blocks and count them. You will need a cornerstone in the row sashing where the block and row sashing meet.

Once you have the dimensions set, cut your sashing strips and cornerstones.

Cornerstone Sashing

This example uses 2 ½" strips for the sashing and 2 ½" squares for the cornerstones, which means that your strip widths are cut at 5" wide and your cornerstones are 5" x 3 ½ rectangles.

9. Sash as usual between the blocks in each row and at each end of the row.

Do not join the rows yet.

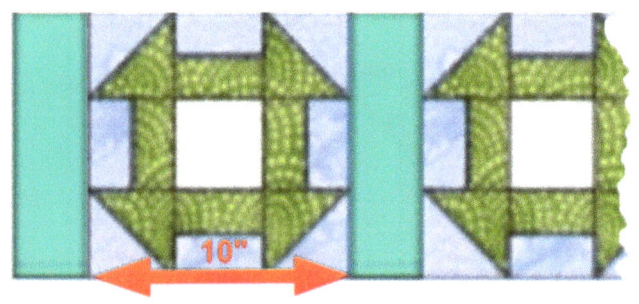

1. Measure carefully the distance between the right side (at the bottom) of the first block in row 1, and the start of the sashing between block 1 and block 2 - add ½ for the ½ seam.".

2. Cut the strip of sashing.

3. Start making the cornerstone sashing strip by sewing a cornerstone piece at the beginning. Join it to the first 10" piece, sewing with a ¼" seam. Sew the next cornerstone to the other end with a ¼" seam.

4. Cut the next strip, this time adding on ¼" as there is only one seam.

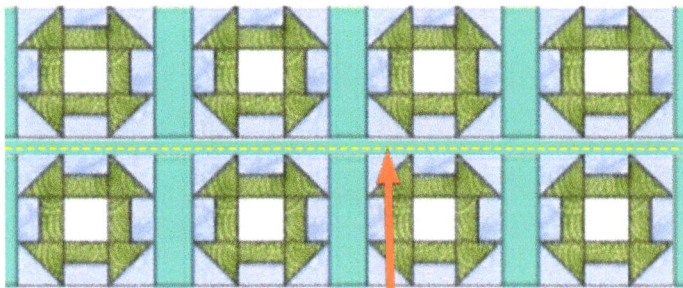

5. Join it to the second cornerstone with a ¼" seam. Continue, repeating the measuring, cutting and sewing until the cornerstone at the end of the row is sewn.

6. Join the backings of row 1 and row 2 and per the QAYG instructions.

7. Open out the rows.

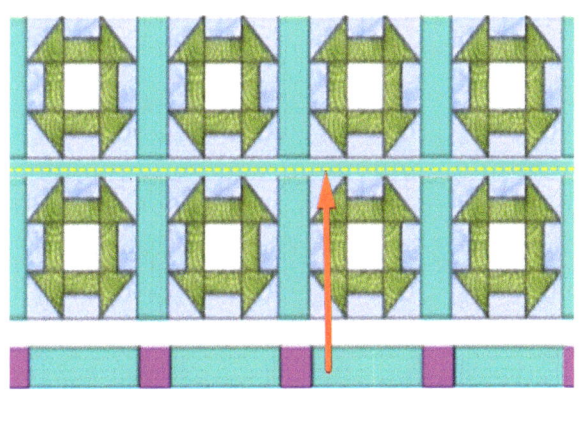

8. Using forked pins or Roxanne Glue(I use both) to keep fabrics from shifting, stitch the sashing over the join of row 1 and the top of row 2.

9. Carefully match the cornerstones to the dividing block sashing in each row.

10. Repeat to assemble a middle section from section rows 3 & 4.

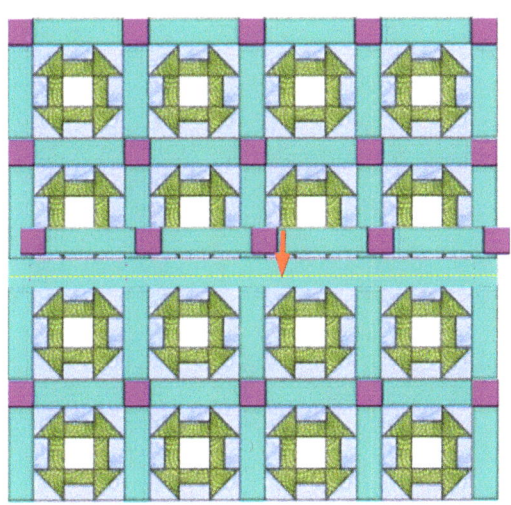

11. Create a bottom section from rows 5 and 6.

12. Use the same joining method attach the top section formed by rows to the middle section.

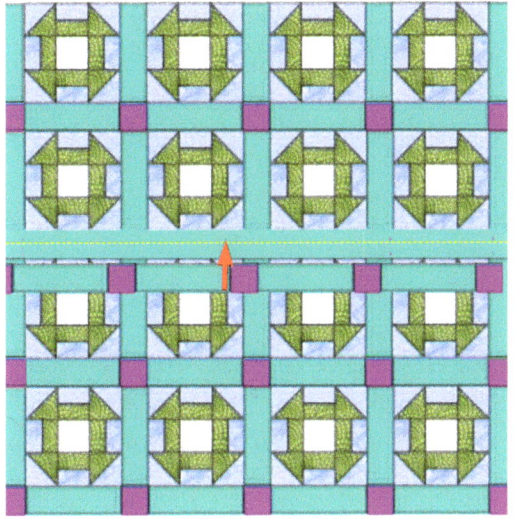

13. Then, using the same process, join the bottom section (rows 5 & 6) to the bottom of the middle section.

14. Sew cornerstone sashing across the top row.

15. Press the quilt.

You are ready for binding.

In conclusion

Quilt As You Go is by far the most comfortable, sensible and pain avoiding method to use for older quilters. Its advantages are;

- Does away with the need to manipulate large lengths and widths of fabric and batting at the cutting stage.
- There is the option to cut for one block, a few blocks or all blocks at a time, reducing the amount of time spent using the rotary cutter and standing at or bending over a cutting table.
- Avoids the need to bend and stretch to bast a quilt top, batting and backing together,
- No need to crawl around the floor to layout a quilt - and then try to get up again.
- Rolling and manhandling large quilts through the machine to quilt is unnecessary.

QAYG gives every quilter the opportunity to develop their free motion quilting skills by starting with controlled quilting and moving onto free motion block quilting and eventually, if they wish to free motion quilting on a longarm quilting machine and frame.

Turn to the section on Quilting for further information.

Quilting

Come out of the ditch!

Why quilt?

A quilt without quilting is just a blanket. It's also unstable. The purpose of quilting is to secure the three layers so that they do mot move when washed or over time and to provide a decorative finish to the quilt. There are many different ways and patterns we can apply to quilting. It can be a "stitch in the ditch" pattern, an all over straight line or meandering path or an intricate feather, loop, trailing vine or other fancy pattern. It can be stitched by hand, or by machine,. If by machine it can be stitched by the quilter guiding the sandwich through the machine, or automatically using a built in stitch on a domestic sewing machine or a pattern built into a longarm machine with an automatic computer controlled application doing the work for you.

There are some quilting methods that become more difficult as we age. Wrangling a double, queen or king size bed quilt onto a table and through a sewing machine can be almost impossible for someone with back, hip or shoulder weakness or deterioration. However, there are ways to quilt that make this final and most creative stage of quilting easier and more rewarding, and more importantly pain-less (we can't guarantee painless, but it will be less pain),

For us, the easiest process in quilting is Quilt-As-You-Go; quilting each block one at a time.

Let's look at that process first, as it is the standard quilting process all quilters use, but on a smaller scale. Whatever steps you follow here, you can apply them to a large bed quilt with a top of pieced and joined blocks, a bed size piece of batting and a single backing. Each block is a "mini-quilt" and each process is equally important to the quality of your finish, so don't rush them.

There are three steps to follow in the quilting of your project;

1. Preparation

2. Basting

3. Quilting

Preparation

First, it is very important that all three layers of the sandwich are smooth and wrinkle free. Iron the backing fabric and lay on the cutting board face down. Carefully pull the fabric taught, don't stretch it, and tape it to the flat surface.

Smooth the batting and lay your block top over the batting. I like to press them both together to get all wrinkles out. It also helps the quilt top stick slightly to the batting. Place the top and batting together on top of the block backing, face up, smooth all wrinkles out. Make sure you can see backing fabric around all four edges of the block top. You sandwich is made. When top and batting are smooth, it's time to baste.

Basting

Using bent safety pins, pin the block top starting at the centre. Working outwards towards the edge, pin every few inches, especially at the edges.

When the pins are in place, remove the tape and check the block back to make sure things are tight and flat. If there are puckers or excess fabric, now is the time to fix the problems. If the fabric is loose when you start quilting, there will be tucks or puckers in the quilting. There is no way to adjust the back once you start sewing without a lot of headaches or time with the seam ripper.

Quilting

There are many options for machine quilting. The first is to let the seams themselves be your guide. Sewing next to the seams themselves is called 'stitch in the ditch.' It works well. If you want to create a more interesting and artistic quilt, you can stitch lines or patterns all over the block or inside the shapes in the block.

There are lots of pre-markers to draw a pattern before you quilt. Pens with disappearing ink, chalk pencils etc. are great, but research the pens you use. Check reviews. Some are harder to get out of fabric than others.

I like to use a Hera marker which gently scores the fabric. You can use a ruler for marking straight lines or there are quilting stencils available in all kinds of patterns. Or be creative.

Marking up your block is easy. While it is on the cutting board, decide how you want to quilt it. Decide whether you will;

- straight line quilt, controlled quilt or free motion quilt.
- use a quilting/creative stitch built into your sewing machine, meander, shadow quilt or trace a pattern from a stencil.

Let's look at these choices and what's involved.

Straight line quilting

Straight line quilting is very easy. You are sewing in a straight line and the machine does all the work moving the needle to create the line.

To make it quicker and easier to have even spaces between the lines, use a marker or a chalk pencil and a ruler or template. There are many templates available to help you mark a straight-line pattern on your blocks or quilts.

Straight line quilting doesn't mean it has to be a boring line of straight sewing. You can have a wavy line as long as it moves through the quilt on a straight line track.

I'm fortunate enough to have some quilting patterns on my sewing machine that are great for straight-line quilting.

It's a good idea to begin quilting from the centre of the block and work out.

I use a walking foot when I'm quilting straight lines. You don't have to have one, but it helps feed the layers of fabric evenly through the machine.

Controlled quilting
The step before free-motion quilting

Many, many new quilters and almost as many old chooks are terrified pf Free Motion quilting. When the feed dogs are down, and all that controls the quilting is your two hands moving the block through the machine, trying to keep to pattern lines while controlling the sewing speed and the stitch length take s a LOT of practice! And a lot of unpicking, tears and tantrums.

The best lesson I ever learnt about quilting was from Pauline Rogers, the best way to practice is without thread. It really is! When you don't have to worry about thread and unpicking stitches you can practice and go back over and over again until you get it right.

Now Pauline has come up with a quilting method that I believe is the middle step in learning to quilt on a domestic sewing machine, which, let's face it, is what most Home Based Quilters have. She calls it Controlled Quilting. The machine controls the stitching, you control the path.

I'll describe it for you - but I suggest you go to Pauline's videos on templates and controlled quilting. She has designed template sets to use with Controlled Quilting and can teach it much better than I. Anyway, this is how it works. I'm still practicing but I love it!!!

There is one catch - you need to have a sewing machine on which you can control the pressure on the presser foot. Forget all your tension dials! We're not talking about tension, we're talking about pressure - how hard your presser foot comes down on the fabric.

I have a Janome Horizon 8900QVP. To change the pressure on the presser foot ,I have to go to a dial on the top of the machine, normally have set at 5.

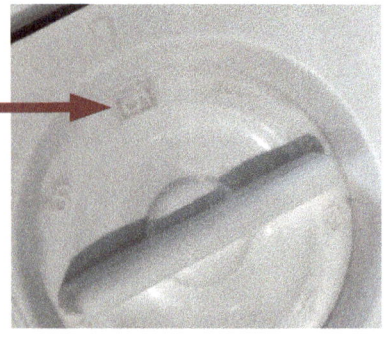

To drop the pressure for Controlled Quilting I turn the dial to its lowest setting - 1. Stitch a stitch and backstitch or two, turn the dial to 2 and then start quilting.

Your machine may have a dial on the side, or you may have to open a door on the left side of the machine housing. If you have a computerised machine you may have to use a setting in your digital control panel.

You need to get to know your machine really well and find your setting. Get out your manual. If you can't find a way to lower the pressure on the presser foot in the manual, talk to your local brand dealer. It may be that you can't lower the pressure at all. In our retirement village craft room, the sewing machines are all a recognised brand, great machines, but not one of the 4 machines can be used for controlled quilting because there is no way to lower the pressure.

That being said, assuming you can and have lowered the pressure on the foot, the next step is to fit your knee control bar - the one that lifts your foot off the fabric, and place the foot control pedal under your LEFT foot. You are going to control your stitching using your left foot. You are now ready to take your marked block and start to stitch. Three things you need to remember,

1. DO NOT DROP THE FEED DOGS! With the lower pressure on the fabric, the feed dogs will move the block through the machine for you while you simply guide its direction.

2. Place your hands on the block, or hold the edges carefully, and guide - do not push or pull -the block, keeping the needle on the pattern line.

3. Stitch slowly and concentrate on keeping the needle following the line, the machine will do the rest.

Here's a block I marked up as a practice piece using a template I have used before for free motion. This is a template for a design to fit into a triangle. There are lots of curves and sharp corners.

This is where speed and the knee lift are important. As you go round corners, slow your speed. If you have a speed control on your machine stop stitching before you

start the curve and turn your speed down. You'll soon learn how far. When you get to a corner, stop stitching, use your knee lift to raise the presser foot, turn the block and line it up and start stitching again. Slow and steady, the machine does all the work.

Practice, practice, practice! Without a thread is a good idea and then when you feel confident, thread your needle and practice with thread.

When you have mastered Controlled Quilting, you will feel less apprehensive about dropping the feed dogs and free motion quilting, mainly because your muscle memory remembers how the fabric moves. It becomes automatic.

The best advice I have for anyone who wants to give controlled quilting a go, is to watch Pauline Rogers' videos. They are an excellent learning resource.

Go to YouTube

https://www.youtube.com/watch?v=HoVuFqQxysw or to Pauline's website

http://www.pqw.com.au

and find her video on the templates and controlled quilting.

Quilting templates and rulers have been designed to make straight line quilting and controlled quilting easy and quick. They are a resource that old chooks and roosters and newbies can make great use of.

However, most old chooks are on a fixed, and sometimes finite, income. We have to make our financial resources and pensions last for the rest of our lives.

While all quilters constantly use their cutters, rulers and markers, and need to have personal tools for every day use, specialist quilting templates and rulers are used only to mark up finished blocks and may be in the cupboard for long periods. They are an ideal for sharing. Quilting groups have a wonderful opportunity to create a "library" of these resources.

Quilt raffles and craft fairs are good fund raisers and can be put to great use.

Free motion quilting

Free motion quilting is joining the layers of a quilt together freehand, using a continuous line of stitching. Imagine your needle is the pen and your quilt is the paper. It's like doodling with your sewing machine needle.

What's the best sewing machine for free motion quilting?

Good news: you don't need a specialist quilting machine to do free motion quilting. You can use the technique on most domestic sewing machines.

If you're looking to buy a new machine, keep an eye out for features that make quilt-making easier. Most machines (though not all cheaper ones) give you the option to lower the feed dogs (more on what that means later).

It's also helpful if sewing machines come with a free motion quilting or darning foot, and extendable or large surfaces for you to rest the quilt on as you sew.

Most sewing machine companies offer models that are designed especially for quilters. These should include everything you need for free motion quilting and more.

How do I free motion quilt?

There are two ways of free motion quilting (FMQ).

- The first involves you manoeuvring the block or quilt through the machine with your hands doing all the work.

- The second involves mounting the block or quilt on a frame and you manoeuvring the machine on a gliding platform allowing it to follow the pattern you have traced. We'll get to quilting frames in a minute or two. For now, let's look at how FMQ happens on your sewing machine at home without a frame.

While, this is is a QAYG approach, substituting the word "quilt" for "block" in the instructions gives you the same process to FMQ a whole bed quilt or large project in one go. Quilting a whole project means moving a lot more weight through a small space, not to mention rolling and folding the part you aren't actively working on. For old chooks and roosters this can be a painful, difficult process so we'll use the block by block approach.

You will need;

- **darning foot** - sometimes referred to as an open toe foot. There is always a spring on the base to allow the foot to travel in all directions when quilting. There are a variety of feet and it may be worthwhile experimenting to see what works best for you. Consult your manual for which does what. If you don't have one, there are universal darning feet available from your local quilt shop or craft supermarket.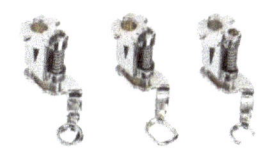

- **walking foot**
- **quilt extension table** for your sewing machine - this is so that the left hand is at the same height as the right when guiding fabric through the sewing machine. You may have one supplied with your sewing machine, or it may be an optional extra.
- **quilting slider mat** - available from most quilting supplies shops, the slider mat has a hole in the middle that goes over the feed dogs and under the presser foot. The underneath is non slip and covers your quilting extension table, allowing the sandwich to slide easily around on the surface. I leave mine on my extension table all of the time. Love it!
- **quilting gloves** - a pair of cotton gloves with non skid pads on the end of the fingers. They give you a great grip on the fabric as you manipulate it through the machine.
- **paper and pencil for doodling** - practice makes perfect in FMQ as you will see.
- **COURAGE AND PERSISTANCE**

Before you start

Plan and play. Think about the pattern or shapes that you want to make when you're quilting. Some quilters prefer to go completely freehand. They move the quilt around in their sewing machine to form loosely sewn shapes, such as stippling, wavy lines or spirals. Others like to trace templates, stencils or rulers to draw the pattern on the fabric.

Whichever you prefer, whichever pattern you choose, before you proceed to fabric and thread, practice, practice, practice with pen and paper until your muscle memory is such that you can doodle the pattern with your eyes closed.

By practice drawing it out by hand, over and over again, your mind and hand will become more comfortable with the design so when your quilt is under the needle you will instinctively know how the pattern forms.

Step 1 Mark where you want your lines to go before you sew.

Place a stencil/template on top of your block and trace the pattern using a fabric marker. Air erasable or water erasable pens, chalk pens and pencils are all handy for this stage. Move the stencil along and repeat, tiling the pattern until you have traced a guideline across a full width of your quilt block.

Test your fabric marker, and how to removable it is, before you cover your quilt in it! I find chalk pencils and pens are less likely to leave marks behind.

Step 3 Select a starter spot on your block.

If you are quilting an all-over pattern, start in the centre of the block, and split it into four-quarter sections. As you sew, move outwards towards the edges of your quarter section. With pin basting, your fabric is more likely to shift and bunch up slightly as you sew. If you start each section at the central point and sew outwards towards the edges, it won't matter if your layers shift a bit as you sew, as you'll have room around the edge to adjust them. They won't end up bunching in the middle of the quilt.

Step 4 Set up your machine and block ready to sew

Drop your feed dogs.

Set your needle to the up position.

Move your fabric underneath the needle, with the start spot in the centre of the free-motion foot's hole. Take the tail of the needle thread between your thumb and first finger and hold it. Lower your needle into the fabric. Carefully lower the foot and raise the needle. The top thread will draw the bottom thread through the fabric. Carefully grasp the bobbin thread and pull a few inches out of the fabric. Draw both the threads together below and to the rear of the foot.

Step 4 Time to sew

Place your hands on the block, close to the edges, either side of the presser foot. Sew a stitch or two back and forth using your machine's reverse stitching setting to secure your thread.

Start sewing your layers together. Sew the beginning of your line by gently pressing the foot to bring your needle up and down. As you sew, move the quilt around with your hands to draw a pattern of freehand stitches with your needle.

The amount of pressure you put on the presser foot, and how fast you move the quilt as you sew, will create your stitch length. Speed up or slow down how much pressure you apply to the foot pedal, and how quickly you move the quilt, to increase or decrease your stitch length.

If your stitches are too long, apply more pressure on the foot pedal and decrease the movement of the quilt. If your stitches are too small, reduce the pressure on your foot pedal and increase the movement of the quilt.

Step 5 Check your tension

After you've stitched a trail of a few inches, stop and check your tension, both above and below your stitching. Look for any "teeth" or signs of wrong tension. If necessary, adjust your tension to create an even line of stitches on both the top and bottom of your block. Check both the underside and the top of your block at the beginning of free motion quilting to ensure that you have balanced the tension.

Step 6 Sew the rest of your block.

If you have used safety pins, remove the pins as you sew. Keep moving across it in sections, blocks or rows, filling each row with your quilted pattern. Sew one section at a time of your block this way. Where you are sewing wavy lines or a stippled pattern, try to sew in one continuous line, without crossing over a previous line you have sewn. However, don't stress if you cross the line, free motion quilting is very forgiving. Nobody will notice it.

When you finish quilting a quarter section, or the whole block, draw the block away from the needle until you have a enough length of needle thread on the top and bobbin thread on the bottom of the sandwich to thread a sewing needle. Cut the threads, leaving enough thread in the machine needle to continue sewing.

Tug the top thread until the bobbin thread follows it and with a pin or your seam ripper, gently draw the bottom thread to the top. Tie the threads off, thread them through a sewing needle and bury them beneath the top fabric, inside the quilt. Now move your block back so the needle is in the centre again to start the next section.

Step 7 Change your bobbin thread when necessary

Before you quilt, always fill a couple of extra bobbins with your matching thread. If you are in the middle of quilting when your bobbin thread runs out, stop sewing and remove the block from the machine. Trace your line of stitching back to where the thread ran out. Gently tug the last few stitches out until you have enough length in your thread ends to knot them off and sew them into the layers of your quilt. Knot them and sew the knot into the layers when you sew your ends into the block.

To stitch again, change the bobbin and pull the new bobbin thread through to the top. Place your block in position at the point at which the line of stitching ended and do several stitches in the same place to secure the thread. Then, off you go again! This allows you to create a variety of patterns and shapes as you sew, or to switch to different thread colours, adding interest to your finished quilt.

For QAYG quilts, when you have a sashed a row of blocks, FMQ or straight line quilting can be used to add interest to and stabilise the sashing both between the blocks and between the rows.

Quilting frames

Whether you enjoy hand quilting or want to speed up your next machine quilting project, a quilting frame makes a great addition to any crafting room. But what exactly do these frames do, and what sort of benefits do they offer and what type is the best quilting frame?

What Are Quilting Frames?

A quilting frame is a structure that holds all three parts of the quilt:and keeps the quilt taut as you work. Frames are used with hand quilting and also with machine quilting. They are made of metal, wood, or plastic. For many quilters, frames are a helpful tool, particularly if they have difficulty laying out and manipulating larger projects. For those of us coping with ageing bodies, quilting block by block on a frame can be a brilliant solution.

While there are several types of quilting frames available, with some designed for hand quilting and others for machine quilting, I'm only going to look at frames suitable for use with both domestic sewing machines and longarm quilting machines.

Domestic Sewing Machines

Types of machine:

Manufacturers design these frames for use with both mid-arm and short-arm machines. They vary in price depending on the style and size of the frame, but even the smallest frame is an expense that needs careful consideration.

- Short Arm machines have a throat space of less than approximately 25cm or 10 inches. While we can use short arm sewing machines on a frame, there is too little throat space for effective use and therefore it is not a worthwhile purchase.

- Mid Arm machines have a throat space ranging from 25 - 38cm or 10 to 15 inches. Mid-arm quilt machines offer the ability to quilt larger patterns or blocks than standard sewing machines.

Long Arm Machines

Most machine quilters are familiar with long arm machines. A long arm frame is typically very large and features an industrial style build. They hold the batting and fabric layers together, making it easier to work on larger projects. The frames usually work with a long arm sewing machine. The machine stitches as the frame unrolls more of the quilt to work on a new section. No basting is necessary.

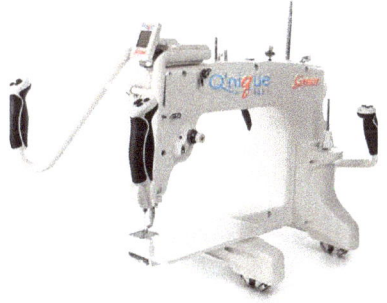

In the past couple of years, smaller frames have become available that can be used with both domestic machines and longarm machines, depending on the throat space available on the machine.

These frames are ideal for home-based quilters whose ability to free motion or straight line quilt is restricted because of reduced hand strength and flexibility or those who suffer from shoulder and back issues and find lifting large quilts too painful.

Unfortunately, some of the smaller frames can only be purchased as a package in conjunction with a table and sewing machine, which makes them unable to be used with your domestic machine.

Larger frames can hold a king-size quilt, some smaller ones can also take large projects but frequently re-setting the quilt on the frame and quilting in "zones" is necessary. However, for QAYG, a smaller frames and your domestic machine is fantastic!!

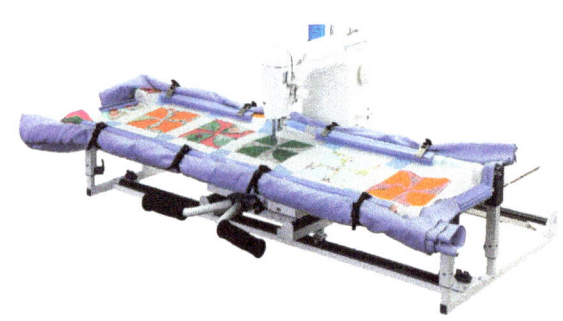

We have a Grace Co "Cutie" frame in our retirement village. Quilters can use the frame on the sewing machines in the craft room, or make a booking to take "Cutie" home and quilt on their own machine. It is light and easily moved, small enough to fit on a dining room table or breakfast bar and will take most domestic machines. The criteria - a base that's less than 11½" thick and there should be no more that 19" of throat space. *There is a list of compatible machines available, but we have found some machines, e.g. Juki TL 2200QVP Mini, have too narrow a throat space to make it worthwhile for older quilters. The effective 6" of quilting space results in too frequent re-setting of the block/quilt for our limited mobility and strength.*

The Benefits of Using Quilting Frames

- Frustration free quilting - Quilting can be challenging. Frames keep the quilt taut as you work to prevent bunching and allow for a more professional look.

- Quicker, less painful finishing of a project - Frames hold all three layers in place and keep the quilt or block taut. Because you're not constantly moving and turning the block as you work, you can complete projects in less time.

- Possibility of Hands-Free Quilting - Advanced mid and long arm machines often have computerised models that will take care of the stitching for you. The result is a professional quilt that requires virtually no hands-on work from the quilter. This is an expensive option, VERY expensive. However, many quilters feel the help and convenience offered by automatic quilting machine and frame makes it well worth the cost.

Using a Quilting Frame

The difference between free motion quilting on your machine with a frame, and free motion quilting on your machine without a frame, is in how you drive it. On your sewing machine, you drive by pushing the fabric through the machine. On a frame, you drive by moving the machine along the fabric. Think of our doodling practice. On the machine, the fabric is the pencil. On a frame, the needle is the pencil.

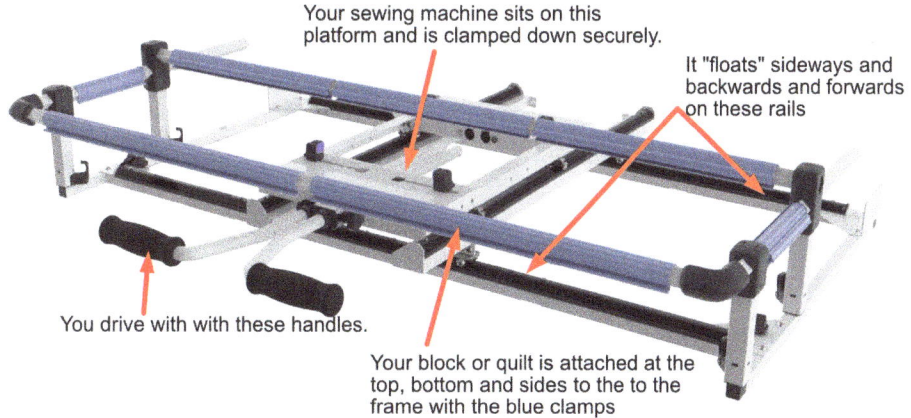

The machine floats on a platform. You can move it with one finger, drive it with one hand. If you choose to have a stitch regulator, the machine will control the stitch speed and length, and stop when you stop moving the machine. You are in control and the physical effort is minimal - until you have to lift the quilt on or off the machine, or roll it on to quilt the next row. With blocks, the effort of moving the fabric is also minimal.

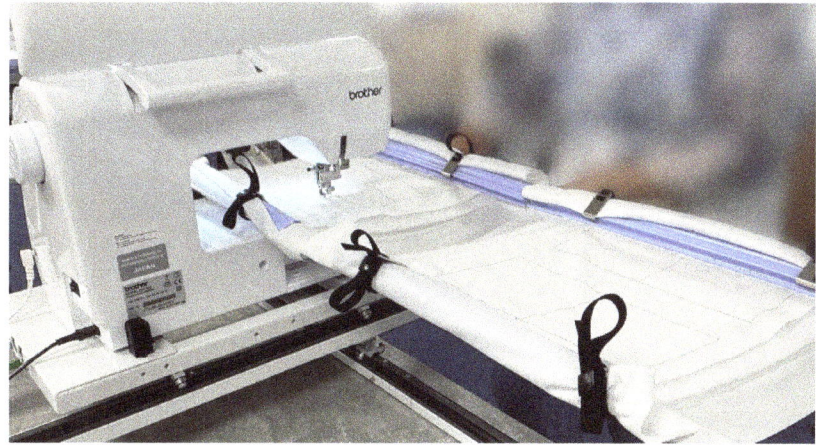

This a Grace Co Cutie frame, with a domestic machine on board. The principle is the same for all small frames. However, follow the instructions that come with your quilting frame and your machine to set up and prepare both machine and frame for quilting. There will be tension, threading and stitch length to be adjusted on your machine, and feed dogs to drop. The quilt or block will have to be mounted on the frame correctly. Take it step by step and go slowly.

Here are some general hints.

- Choose a comfortable chair when working with a frame. Armless chairs with rollers are a good choice. Arms should be parallel to the floor.
- Always work from one side to the other—either right or left.
- Always stitch toward yourself, rather than away from yourself.

For QAYG ;

- Prepare your blocks as usual.
- Use a 12" top leader and a 24" bottom leader. Some small frames have leaders for front and back rails as an accessory, or you can make your own from calico. Leaders give you extra length to roll around the top rail, allowing you to start quilting at the edge of the block.
- Pin or baste top edge of the block backing to the top leader and the bottom edge of the block to the bottom leader.
- Mount your block on the frame according to the manufacturer's instructions.

If working on a quilt;

- Make sure the back is 6" longer than the top and the batting 4"- 5" longer than the top.
- Lay the quilt backing face down on the floor or a flat surface, and place the batting over the backing followed by the quilt top. You can choose to sew or baste your layers together, but it's unnecessary.
- Have a friend help you load the frame. Trying to load a full quilt on the machine by yourself can be difficult, if not painful.
- Use flower head pins when using frames with rollers. You can turn these pins to lie down flat, thus avoiding lumps in the fabric as you roll.
- Always mark your pattern on the top before you load the block/quilt.

A final word on quilting

So many quilters are apprehensive about quilting. Many go no further than stitch in the ditch, and few tackle free motion quilting any further than meandering or stippling. With the right tools, and a helping hand, you can create beautiful, professional standard quilted projects.

Whether you straight line quilt, controlled quilt or free motion quilt, there are so many resources to help you. YouTube has many helpful videos, as do Pauline's Quilter's World and Leah Day's website. Grace Co has an HBQ Community website with an infinite amount of information to get you started.

Give it a go. You won't regret it.

Useful Stuff

Useful websites and online stores for Aussie quilters

1. Grace Co - Rulers and cutters for those with weak or arthritic hands &quilting machines

    https://graceframe.com/en

2. Grace Co Australian Distributor - Know How Sewing Essentials

    https://knowhowsewing.com.au

3. Pauline's Quilters World - templates, how to's and quilting tools.

    https://pqw.com.au/

4. Adobe Colour

    https://color.adobe.com/create/color-wheel

5. Punch With Judy - reliable online supplier with a wide range of quilting tools

    https://www.punchwithjudy.com.au/

6. The Fabric Patch - reliable online supplier with a wide range or pre-cuts, especially Moda.

    https://fabricpatch.com.au

Quilting Calculators

1. **Robert Kaufman QuiltingCalc** Quilting calculator - Google Play or Apple Store

2. **Quilters Paradise website** - https://www.quiltersparadiseesc.com/Calculators.php

3. **The Strawberry Thief website** - https://thestrawberrythief.com.au/fabric-calculators/

If you are interested in reading the reports on quilting as a benefit to health and well being, they are available online at;

Ian M. McDonough, Sara Haber, Gérard N. Bischof, and Denise C. Park. "The Synapse Project: Engagement in Mentally Challenging Activities Enhances Neural Efficiency,"Restorative Neurology and Neuroscience, Volume 33, Issue 6 (2015), DOI: 10.3233/RNN-150533, published by IOS Press. Texas

Emily L. Burt, Jacqueline Atkinson, The relationship between quilting and wellbeing, Journal of Public Health, Volume 34, Issue 1, March 2012, Pages 54–59, https://doi.org/10.1093/pubmed/fdr041 Glasgow

Glossary of Terms

A

Amish Quilts

These are quilts made by or in the style of the Amish quilters of the USA. For example, the geometric patterns and central medallion square-in-a-square quilts with wide borders is a common pattern in Amish communities.

Appliqué

A piece of fabric sewn on top of a background piece of fabric. For example curved floral or animal motifs. Appliqué can be sewn by hand, machine, or attached with fusible web. I

Art Quilt

Art quilts use both traditional and modern quilting technique. They may combine patchwork, appliqué, embroidery, and more.

Attic Window Quilt Pattern

An optical illusion quilt pattern that makes it appear as though you're looking at each quilt block through a window.

Autograph Quilt

A quilt containing signatures from friends or others, often for celebrating an important life event.

B

Backing

The back layer of a quilt, which is not pieced or appliquéd.

Bargello

A type of quilt that creates movement by how the strips of fabric squares are sewn, usually of the same colour going from light to dark.

Basting

Long, temporary stitches used to hold layers of fabric together (loosely) until the final sewing is done. The stitches are removed when the quilt is completed.

Batting

The middle layer of the quilt (between the quilt top and back) that provides the warmth to the quilt. Types of batting are usually made from cotton, polyester, and wool.

Bearding

The migration of fibres coming from the batting and passing through the quilt top, usually via the holes where the needle pierces through the quilt top.

Betweens

Short and thin needles that are used for hand piecing and quilting as well as sewing on the binding. The size of the needles range from 7-12, with the higher number indicating a smaller needle.

Bias

The bias grain runs at a 45° angle to the selvedges and has an amount of stretch, making it less stable than the lengthwise and crosswise grain. Be extremely careful, as cutting on the bias grain may cause inaccurate cuts.

Bias Binding

Binding cut on the true bias. This is useful when binding a quilt that has curved or rounded corners.

Big Stitch

A type of quilting where colourful thread is used to make large stitches, creating a decorative effect.

Binding

A strip of fabric sewn over the edges of the finished quilt. Binding adds extra strength and support.

Blind Stitch

Invisible stitching often used for sewing appliqué or binding by hand. Blind stitch can also be done on a sewing machine.

Block

A quilt design is generally made up of multiple squares that are repeated and sewn together to make a quilt top.

Block of the Month (BOM)

Projects/subscriptions offered by quilting classes or quilt shops. Each month Quilters are supplied the materials to make a new block. At the end of a year, the blocks are joined to make a quilt top. You can find many BOM clubs or memberships online or even in quilt patterns.

Border

A strip of fabric that frames a quilt. It usually forms part of the quilt top. Borders can be wide or narrow depending on your project.

Broadcloth

A plain weave cotton blend of sturdy fabric, typically solid in colour.

C

Calico
Medium-weight cotton fabric, which may be plain, flecked or printed with a small repeated design, often consisting of leaves or florals.

Cathedral Window
A traditional quilt pattern. Folding and stitching is used to create a quilt block with a three-dimensional look. Cathedral Window blocks are intricate and elegant.

Charm Quilt
A type of scrappy quilt made with a lot of small patches . Each piece of fabric is different. Charm quilt patterns are generally a one-patch design. Quilters sometimes trade fabric scraps to collect a variety of fabric for their charm quilt. This is where pre-cut "Charm Squares" got their name.

Cheater Cloth
Fabric printed to looks like a traditionally pieced quilt top. It removes the need for cutting and piecing and can be sandwiched and quilted in one piece.

Clamshell
A quilt with curves that overlap in rows like fish scales. You can create the clamshell design by using a glass or cup to trace the fish scale shape..

Coin Quilt
A scrappy quilt made with rectangular fabric pieces that are arranged in stacks around the quilt.

Colour Wheel
A circle of primary, secondary, tertiary, complementary, and analogous colours that help quilters to explore colour theory and fabric selection.

Corner Triangles
Half square triangles, usually sewn on to square up and stabilise a quilt top made from blocks that are joined in diagonal rows.

Crazy Quilt
An irregular quilt consisting of odd shapes, randomly placed.and enhanced with embellishments such as lace, embroidery or beading.

Cross-Hatching
Quilting in parallel lines, vertical and horizontal, forming a grid of squares or diamonds.

D

Design Wall
A vertical surface used by quilters to lay out fabrics and blocks for a quilt before stitching them together to practice layouts.

Disappearing Nine Patch
A beginner's quilt made by cutting up a nine patch into four quarters, putting them into different positions, and piecing the blocks over again.

Double Wedding Ring
A vintage quilt pattern of interlocking rings. It has been around since the 1930s and is still a great favourite.

Dresden Plate
An appliqué quilt with wedged shapes radiating from a centre circle. Dresden Plate is one of the most popular blocks from the 1920s and 30s.

Drunkard's Path
A classic quilt block pattern. It consists of a quarter circle set inside a square, using light and dark for each. Arranged blocks differently can create several designs.

E

Easing
The process of gently manipulating the fabric to match at the seams when two pieces a don't align correctly.

Echo Quilting
A free motion type of quilting around an appliqué by stitching a line a uniform distance away from the first line. The quilting lines then echo the appliqué's shape.

English Paper Piecing
A technique used to stabilise a fabric piece by stitching it over a paper template. It's often used for pieced patterns that would otherwise require set-in patches.

F

Fat Quarter (FQ)
A half yard of fabric that has been cut in half again vertically and is now ¼" yard, measuring 18" x 22" and allows for cutting larger block sizes. A metric Fat Quarter is 110cm x 25cm

Feed Dogs
The metal teeth on the throat plate of a sewing machine which pulls the fabric through the machine.

Finger Pressing
Using your fingernail and pressing hard on a seam to make it lie flat. It works best on small seams as opposed to larger ones.

Finished Size
The final sewn measurement or dimensions of a completed quilt block without seam allowances.

Flannel

A soft type of loosely woven fabric usually made from cotton, wool or synthetic fibres and is very warm. It's great for rag quilts because of its tendency to ravel.

Flying Geese

A patchwork unit made by piecing two smaller triangles onto the sides of a larger triangle to create a rectangular piece of patchwork. The finished unit looks like the shape formed by a flock of geese flying in formation.

Foundation Piecing

The technique of using a Muslin pattern or numbered paper as a foundation for assembling a quilt block, which ensures accurate and stable blocks.

Four-Patch Block

A block with four squares of the same size sewn together to make one large square. It is one of easiest quilt blocks to make. A variation of this block is the Vanishing Four Patch. A completed four patch block is cut in a specific way and the pieces rearranged to make a new, very attractive pattern.

Freezer paper appliqué

The process of using freezer paper as a template for appliqué by drawing the design on the paper side, cutting it out, and ironing the template to the fabric using a hot and dry iron.

Free-Motion Quilting

Quilting on a domestic sewing machine by dropping the feed dogs down, and using a darning foot to quilt in different directions, creating a variety of stitch patterns.

Friendship Quilt

A single pattern quilt made by a group of friends and/or family for one person. Each makes a block for the quilt top and includes their signature. It is also referred to as a Signature Quilt.

Friendship Star

A quilt block pattern that looks like a four-pointed star.

Fusible Web Interfacing

An iron on webbing for easier appliqué by providing great support to the fabric.

Fussy Cut

Cutting a particular piece from printed fabric to get a the specific image you need.

Glass-head pins

Pins with a glass head that is heat resistant. They don't melt when pressed.

Grain

The lengthwise and crosswise threads, (warp and weft) of a woven fabric. The lengthwise grain runs parallel to the selvedge, with the least amount of stretch. The crosswise grain runs perpendicular to the selvedge and has slightly more give.

H

Half-Square Triangle (HST)
A 90 degree triangle formed when a square is cut in half one time diagonally.

Hanging Sleeve
Fabric sewn to the back of a quilt to allow it to be hung on a wall or to be put on display at a quilt show or other event.

Hera
A small tool from Japan made of wood or plastic. It allows you to put a crease in the fabric, replacing the need to draw a line and ensuring success with straight-line quilting.

Herringbone Stitch
A decorative needlework stitch with many variations used in embroidery.

Homespun Fabric
Fabric in which the weave is looser and the threads have a larger diameter than commercial cotton quilting fabrics. Easily identified as there is no front or back. The coloured threads are woven throughout.

Hopping Foot
A special sewing foot for quilting used when you want greater visibility on your stitching.

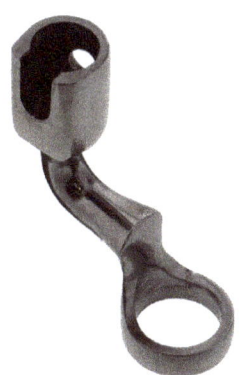

I

In-The-Ditch
Stitching along the seams in a quilt in order to define blocks or shapes. Also known as stitch-in-the ditch.

Irish Chain
A classic quilt pattern consisting of several variations. It is usually made up of squares and strips, and makes a great beginner quilt pattern.

Isosceles Triangle
A triangle with two equal sides whose combined length (the sum of the two equal sides) is longer than the third side.

J

Japanese Quilt
A type of quilt using Japanese fabrics such as kasuri and indigo. Fabrics, motifs, and stitches work together to create a striking quilt.

Jelly Roll
A coordinated bundle of 2 ½" x 44" pre-cut fabric strips, usually from a design collection or of a basic colour. There are 40 strips to a Jelly roll and 20 strips to a junior Jelly Roll.

Juvenile Quilts
A quilt designed and themed for appropriate for children.

Knot on the Needle

A tiny knot that quilters use, pulled through a layer of fabric so that the end is hidden on both sides. Also known as a "quilter's knot."

Label

A way of autographing your quilt. Most labels include the quilter's name, the name of the quilt, and when it was made.

Landscape Quilt

An art quilt depicting the many scenes from nature.

Layer Cake

A bundle of 10" x 10" pre-cut coordinating fabric squares. A versatile option as you can cut smaller pieces from the square or use the square as is.

Layout

Arranging your blocks or pieced units in a quilt top, or rearranging them to create completely different looks.

LeMoyne Star

A distinctive, eight-pointed star block, usually for more advanced quilters.

Loft

A term describing the thickness of the batting used in quilts. High loft batting is usually thick and bouncy, while low loft batting is thinner and more compact.

Log Cabin

A quilt pattern in which narrow fabric strips (logs) are assembled in a numerical sequence around a centre square to form a block. Log Cabin blocks are a popular design and have many variations.

Long Arm Quilting (LAQ)

A large sewing machine with a long arm used to sew together all three layers of the quilt. It allows a quilter to use their free-motion skills moving larger quilts more easily. Longarm machines are used with a quilting frame, allowing the quilter to move the machine across the quilt.

Machine Appliqué

Attaching fabric motifs onto fabric using a sewing machine.

Machine Piecing

Sewing patches together using a machine as opposed to hand piecing.

Machine Quilting

Sewing through all three layers of the quilt top with a sewing machine. It is usually done with a walking foot or a darning foot.

MAQ

Mid-Arm Quilter. Similar to a longarm quilter, but with less space in the throat of the machine.

Matching Points

It is the intersection where a seam line joining two pieces begins or ends.

Medallion Quilt

A series of decorative borders that surrounds one central block or design.

Metallic Needle

A thin needle designed with an elongated eye (for easier threading) for use with metallic or monofilament threads.

Metallic Thread

A synthetic thread that is shiny and has a metallic appearance.

Memory Quilts

Quilts made to remember people and/or an event significant in their lives. The quilts sometimes contain photographs, clothes from a loved one, or items made by that person .

Mercerised Cotton

Cotton thread treated with Sodium Hydroxide (Caustic Soda) to swell the fibres and increase the fibre's lustre and its ability to absorb dye by increasing the surface area. The treatment makes the cotton stronger, is less likely to shrink.

Miniature Quilts

A quilt made as a miniature of a full sized quilt, including mug rugs and potholders among other things.

Mitred Corner

A corner formed when two strips meet at a 45-degree angle, such as on a border or the binding. Mitred corners ensure that the edges of your quilt have neat finish.

Motif

A design element used in quilt designs that can be repeated or used only once.

Mug Rug

A small quilt used as a coaster for your coffee mug.

Muslin

A plain cotton fabric of medium weight that is naturally unbleached. It's available in a wide range of qualities from light to medium weight and delicate to coarse weave..

Mystery Quilt

A quilt pattern written in different steps that are disclosed one at a time in order to hide the appearance of the finished quilt.

N

Nine-Patch

A quilt block consisting of nine squares arranged in three rows horizontally. They are perfect blocks for beginners to make. Similar to Four Patch blocks, when complete they can be sliced and the pieces rearranged and re-sewn to make a wide variety of attractive blocks.

Needle-Punched Batting

The manufacturing method used to make batting more firm and more dense by punching it with a group of needles. Needle punched batting makes quilts more durable.

Needle-Turn Appliqué

A traditional hand appliqué technique in which the seam allowances are turned under as shapes are hand sewn to the background, giving you invisible stitches.

Notches

A tiny "V" shape cut into a curved seam to indicate points along the seam that should be matched. Notches are significantly important when trying to sew curved seams.

Novelty Print

A fabric designed and printed with a theme such as holidays, pets, sports, and so on.

O

One-Patch

Any quilt pattern that uses a single shaped patch for the pieced top. May be squares, triangles, hexagons, etc. repeated in colour patterns or different fabrics.

One Quarter Inch (¼") Quilting Foot

This foot measures exactly one quarter inch from needle point to the edge of the foot. which may have a guide on it preventing the fabric going past the edge. Most sewing machines come with a quilting presser foot. If not, there is a Universal quarter inch foot that will fit most machines.

On Point

The orientation of a quilt when its corners are placed up, down and to the sides.

Outline Quilting

A type of quilting where you outline (stitch) a block or appliqué piece usually ¼" from the patch seams.

Outline Stitch

A decorative stitch used in embroidery that forms a narrow line.

P

Panel Quilt

A quilt made mostly from a pre-printed fabric panel; large pieces of fabric printed with some sort of picture or scene. Fabric panels are ready to use with no need to cut them up for patchwork.

Paper Piecing

Machine stitching your fabric directly onto paper. You can achieve perfect points if you position your fabric correctly and sew perfect straight lines. Also known as Foundation Paper Piecing.

Patchwork

The process of making a quilt by sewing many small pieces of fabric together to create many different designs for a quilt top. Also known as piecework.

Photo Quilt

A personalised quilt made from squares of fabric on which are printed you chosen photograph(s). The quilt is then designed to incorporate the photograph blocks.

Pieced Border

A long strip of fabric that has been sewn together to make a single border for your quilt. Pieced borders can make a vibrant impact on your quilt.

Pinwheel

A common quilt block pattern consisting of four triangles arranged in a pinwheel pattern and sewn into a four-patch block.

Prairie Points

A technique in which you fold strips of fabric in order to form triangles and then use them as a quilt border or embellishment on seams within a quilt. Quilts with Prairie Points don't need binding.

Pre-Cut Fabric

Types of coordinating fabric bundles that are pre-cut by the manufacturer. Charm Packs, Jelly Rolls, Fat Quarters, and Layer Cakes are some examples of pre-cuts.

Presser Foot

The part of the sewing machine that surrounds the needle and keeps the fabric flat against the plate as the needle stitches. There is variety of presser feet, designed for various tasks, available for most sewing machine brands .

Pressing

Using an iron to press seams and blocks by pressing the iron down onto the fabric.The iron shouldn't be too hot, nor should you use steam.

Prewash

Washing your fabrics before using them in a quilt project to preshrink it and ensure that dyes will not bleed in future washings. Most fabrics today do not require pre-washing for shrinking, however, testing for colourfastness on a small piece of fabric is always wise.

Q

Quilting

The process of stitching together the three layers of a quilt.

Quilt Sandwich

The layering of quilt top, batting, and backing quilted together.

Quilt Top

The top layer of a quilt Sandwich.

R

Rag Quilt

A type of piecework with exposed seams on the front and finished seams on the back giving a ragged look. They are assembled differently to traditional quilt.

Raw Edge

The unsewn edge of a piece of fabric or a quilt block sometimes used as a decorative element.

Reverse Appliqué

Appliqué fabric is sewn to the back of the background fabric and then the background fabric is cut away to reveal the appliqué underneath. It is especially useful when the shapes are small and when an illusion of depth is needed.

Rotary Cutter

A tool with a sharp circular blade attached to a handle, used to cut fabric on a cutting mat. It comes in a variety of diameters.

Ruler

A heavy plastic measuring tool available in a variety of shapes and sizes.

S

Sampler Quilt

A quilt constructed of a collection of blocks in different patterns. No pattern is repeated. The Sampler Quilt is perfect for the beginner quilter.

Sashiko Quilting

A Japanese style of precise quilting designs done in embroidery or in quilting and it typically involves using white thread on a dark solid background.

Sashing

The fabric that separates the blocks from each other, framing them and making the quilt larger. In Quilt As You Go, sashing is used after each block has been quilted, to join them into rows and then join the rows to assemble the quilt.

Satin Stitch

A slanted, compact decorative stitch often used around appliqué pieces to finish off raw edges.

Scrap Quilt

A quilt made with a combination of leftover fabrics from other quilts.

Seam Allowance

The width of fabric left to the right of a sewn seam. In quilting this is traditionally ¼ inch.

Selvedge (Selvage)

The outer edge of both sides of a woven fabric where the weft turns to go back across and through the warp. It is a stiffer and denser woven area of about 1/3-½ inch and is usually trimmed off and not sewn into a quilt.

Setting

The arrangement of completed Blocks forming the Quilt Top. Blocks can be set side by side, or on point, like diamonds, with or without Sashing.

Signature Quilt

A quilt with many signatures collected and signed on individual blocks.

Stash

A quilter's collection of fabrics, usually quite an impressive amount.

Stippling

A stitching technique of curved lines that is done all over the quilt to fill in background areas. Stippling allows designs to be seen more prominently in the quilt.

Stitch in the Ditch

A stitch used next to the seams on the quilt in order to define blocks or shapes.

Straight of Grain

The lengthwise and crosswise grain on fabric.

Strip Piecing

Cutting fabric into even width strips and sewing them together accurately and quickly. They are then cut into new blocks and designs.

Sunbonnet Sue

An appliqué design of a girl with a sunbonnet hiding her face. Popular among quilters since the 1920s.

Tacking Gun

A tool used instead of pin or thread basting the quilt sandwich together prior to quilting.

Template

A shape cut from plastic or cardboard and used as a pattern for tracing either piecing or appliqué patches. It may also be used to transfer quilting lines to a quilt top.

Tied Quilt

A quilt in which knotted strings or ties are used to hold the three layers of the quilt together as opposed to stitching.

Trapunto

A quilt that contains shapes stuffed in order to give them and the quilt more dimension. It can be stuffed with yarn, additional batting, or other fabric.

Unfinished Objects (UFOs)

Unfinished quilt projects that you have in your studio. It is common for quilters to have many of them.

Unit

Two or more sections of a block or border that are sewn together.

Utility Quilt

A plain, basic practical use quilt made without fancy materials. It is meant for warmth and for your everyday bedding.

Variegated Thread

Thread used in quilting that changes in colour throughout the strand.

Vertical Row

A quilt arranged vertically as opposed to the more traditional horizontal method. There are some specific designs that will look better if the quilt is assembled vertically.

Walking Foot

Foot attached to a sewing machine that has grippers on the bottom. It helps to feed the quilt through more evenly. It is especially effective to use this walking foot in machine quilting.

Warp

The woven threads in the fabric that run from top to bottom of the weaving loom, and parallel to the selvedges. They are the most stable part of the fabric. Some quilters like to use the warp direction for cutting borders.

Weft

The woven threads in the fabric that run across the loom, through the warp threads. The weft direction is not as stable as the warp.

Water-Soluble

Threads, markers, and stabilisers that dissolve when wet.

Wonky

Imperfect patchwork in which fabrics are cut at awkward angles and sewn together with no rhyme or reason. Often used by quilters with reference to blocks that don't quite turn out as they should!

X-Ray Film

Some quilters use X-Ray film to make templates.

Y-Seams

Joining three different pieces of fabric together to form a "Y". Stop ¼" away from the seam.

Yo-Yo Quilt

A fabric embellishment made with three-dimensional circles. A Yo-Yo tool is available in various sizes from your local quilt shop.

Zipper Quilt

A quilt pieced together to mimic a zipper.

Zigzag Stitch

A stitch that goes from side to side and is used for machine appliqué. The stitches can be short or long, wide or narrow.

www.ingramcontent.com/pod-product-compliance
Lightning Source LLC
Chambersburg PA
CBHW061806290426
44109CB00031B/2944